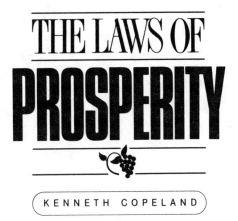

# THE LAWS OF PROSPERITY

KENNETH COPELAND

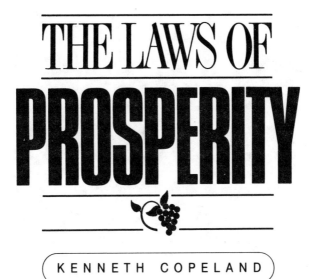

# THE LAWS OF PROSPERITY

( KENNETH COPELAND )

KCP Publications
Fort Worth, Texas

**The Laws of Prosperity**

ISBN 0-8007-0725-7                                        #30-0007

Reprinted June 1990

© 1974 Kenneth Copeland Ministries, Inc.

Unless otherwise indicated, all Scripture quotations are from
the KING JAMES VERSION.

Published by KCP Publications
Fort Worth, Texas 76192

# Contents

*Dedication*

*To my Partners*
*who have been so faithful*
*to support this ministry*

# Introduction

God first began dealing with me about the laws that govern prosperity in 1967. I was conducting a series of meetings in a very small church in a very small town in the Texas Panhandle. For years I had entertained the idea that success was not an accident, that luck has nothing to do with it. I had read books of different kinds on this idea but had not found any answers that satisfied me. It didn't occur to me that the Bible was written by the most successful individual alive—God!

In those early days of following the Lord's teaching, it seemed that He was very hard on me. I could see no reason for Him to be so strict. Of course, I had no idea then that, in less than ten years, prime interest rates would soar to heights as never before. Who could dream that the fuel shortage, food shortage, paper shortage, etc., would come storming their way into our lives.

When Gloria and I first began to put the things we were learning into practice, we had nothing around us but problems. I had returned to college at the age of thirty and from there God called us into a full-time ministry in His service. We were deeply in debt and lived in surroundings that were very poor. The job God called me to do required that I travel extensively preaching and teaching His Word, but our car was completely worn out. We had no clothes. I had lost seventy-five pounds and, obviously, none of my clothes fit. The trousers on some of my suits had been altered so many times that, instead of two back pockets, it looked like one big pocket! I could go on and on about our situation, but it's easy to see that we had less than nothing. We were thousands of dollars in debt.

God used His Word to set the standards by which we would operate. It had to be by faith or not at all. We made commitments that seemed so hard. We declared that we would never ask any man for anything including money and places to minister. We pledged ourselves and this ministry to Romans 13:8, that we would never borrow one cent. We would tell our needs only to God and expect what He was teaching us to produce. Little did we know then what a blessing these standards would be. We learned, many times the hard way. We prayed. We confessed our faith. We stood on God's Word when every circumstance spelled absolute doom. God's Word worked! Things began to happen *for us* instead of *to us*. We began to grow. In eleven months, we were free from debt. Unless you have experienced the freedom of being debt-free, you cannot imagine how great it is not to have any man putting pressure on you. We know what Hebrews 4:11 means when it says, ...*labour therefore to enter into that rest*. There is peace and rest when you know how to operate in God's laws instead of being forced to seek help from men's sources.

God always has *more* than enough. The rise in interest rates has not affected our ministry. The rise in medical costs has not affected us. We have learned to receive our healing from God.

The world's shortages have no effect on someone who has already gone to heaven. Therefore, they should have no effect on us here who have made Jesus the Lord of our lives. Philippians 4:19 says that our needs are to be met according to *His* riches in glory, not *our* shortages in earth. Our problem has been in not knowing heaven's ways of doing things. We have tried to live in God's blessings with the world's laws. It won't work. We receive from God by using His laws and ways.

In the book you are about to read, I have shared these laws of prosperity the way they were given to me from God's Word. They are not theories; they are facts. We have tried and proven each one in our own lives! We live this

# Introduction

way. My invitation to you is from Malachi 3:10. God Himself says, *Prove me now herewith…if I will not open you the windows of heaven, and pour you out a blessing, that there shall not be room enough to receive it.* Determine now to act on God's Word and start looking for *more* room!

*Kenneth Copeland*

# Chapter One
# *The Laws of Prosperity*

As we begin this study of prosperity and how it functions according to the Word of God, let's read the basic scriptures on which our whole study is founded. Let me mention here that we are putting the Word of God first and foremost throughout this study, not what we *think* it says, but what it *actually* says! When we see it in the Word, believe it, and begin to act on it, faith is created. *Faith cometh by hearing, and hearing by the word of God* (Rom. 10:17).

As you read our basic scripture text, remember that Jesus said in John 17:17, *Thy word is truth.* For a clearer meaning substitute *the Word* for *truth* as follows:

*Beloved, I wish above all things that thou mayest prosper and be in health, even as thy soul prospereth. For I rejoiced greatly, when the brethren came and testified of the truth* [the Word] *that is in thee, even as thou walkest in the truth* [the Word]. *I have no greater joy than to hear that my children walk in truth* [the Word] (3 John 2-4).

It would be good to point out that when the apostle John wrote this epistle, he was an old man and had been in the Christian walk for a long, long time – in fact, from the time of his youth. He had walked with Jesus and watched Him closely throughout His earthly ministry. John was a wise old man, strong in the Lord, and he said, "I wish *above all things* that you prosper and be in health."

Through our traditional ideas, we have been lead to believe that prosperity is bad or ungodly. However, John writes that we *should* prosper and be in health and then says in verse 11, *Beloved, follow not that which is evil, but*

11

*that which is good. He that doeth good is of God: but he that doeth evil hath not seen God.* If prosperity is evil, why would He want us to prosper? You see, there is nothing wrong with prosperity in itself. *Money* is not the root of all evil. *The love of money* is the root of all evil (see 1 Tim. 6:10), and there are people committing this sin who don't have a dime! I want you to realize, however, that prosperity covers much more than finances.

When John said we should prosper and be in health, he added the phrase, *Even as thy soul prospereth.* Man is a spirit; he has a soul consisting of the mind, the will, and the emotions; and he lives in a body. Thus, there is *spiritual* prosperity; there is *mental* prosperity; and there is *physical* prosperity.

To prosper spiritually, you must be born again. When you accept Jesus as your Savior and make Him the Lord of your life, your spirit is reborn and brought into fellowship with the Father, the Almighty God. This then puts you in a position to receive from Him *all* the things promised in His Word.

To prosper in your soul, you must be able to *control* your mind, your will, and your emotions. Just because you have accumulated large amounts of knowledge does not mean that your mind is prosperous. Prosperity of the mind comes when you use the knowledge that has been accumulated—when you are controlling your mind instead of your mind controlling you. Second Corinthians 10:5 says we are to cast down imaginations and every high thing that exalts itself against the knowledge of God (or against the Word of God), bringing into captivity every thought to the obedience of Christ. The person who does this has control of his mind and is in position to prosper mentally. *You cannot control your mind completely without the Word of God being alive and operating inside you.*

You must control your will in the same way. Some people say, "Lord, help my will to crumble." God doesn't want a broken will that He can dominate. He wants your will whole and in submission to His will so that the two of you can work together in unity. When God made man, He gave him a will that has power. It is actually a godlike will because man has the right to choose his own eternal destiny. Only a god has that kind of choice! Man was made in God's image and given the will to make up his own mind. You can go to hell if you want to and God will protect your right...you don't have to, but you can. On the other hand, you can choose Jesus Christ and the Word of God. In Deuteronomy 30:19, God said, *I call heaven and earth to record this day against you, that I have set before you life and death, blessing and cursing: therefore choose life, that both thou and thy seed may live.* What a privilege! *The choice is yours!*

When a man's soul is prosperous, his will is in line with God's will. How can you get in line with God's will? You can't until you know what His Word says. His Word and His will are the same! An honest man can't will one thing and say another. *If you are in line with the Word of God, you are in line with the will of God.*

Let's discuss our emotions as part of the soul. The person who is emotionally prosperous can control his emotions. I used to think this meant never showing emotions, but that's not so. Jesus had complete control over His emotions, yet He wept at the tomb of Lazarus! The important thing is that His weeping didn't cause Him to join the grief-stricken throng of people. He continued to move in the Spirit. He put His priorities where they belonged and raised Lazarus from the dead. He showed emotions, but He was not moved by them.

You will never be healthier or more prosperous than your soul. You can be born again, even filled with the Holy Spirit, and still not be prosperous in your soul. For instance, an old saint of God, living in poverty, can pray revival down on a church, get everybody in town saved, and be lying in bed sick the whole time—*if she does not believe the Word of God for her health!* She can do these

13

things, never knowing the fullness of the infilling of the Holy Spirit and speaking with other tongues, even though healing and prosperity belong to her all the time. You see, her soul was not prosperous in these areas; her mind had not grasped the full meaning of the Word of God; her mental computer had never been fed on God's Word concerning healing, the Holy Spirit, and prosperity. She knew the Word enough to seek salvation and revival and used this knowledge to pray down the power of God. Her soul was prosperous in this area.

The world's definition of *physical prosperity* (prosperity of the senses) includes gold, silver, financial favor or power, political favor or power, and social favor or power. The world's definition of *mental prosperity* (prosperity of the soul) is "knowing it all." Put these two ideas together and you have a person who can use his mind to get financial and political power. This is the world's total concept of prosperity. You can easily see its drawbacks! Wealth and power cannot answer every problem. Money makes a lousy god! It can't buy good health or prevent sickness and disease from taking over the human body. Yes, it can go toward buying it, but the world's system of healing just isn't good enough. In the mental realm, a person can have all the facts in his head and not have the ability to use that knowledge to obtain the money or the health that he needs.

What produces spiritual, mental, and physical prosperity? What brings all these areas together? The Word of God. The Bible says in Hebrews 4:12 that the Word is alive, powerful, and sharper than a two-edged sword. It says that it divides the soul and the spirit, the joints and the marrow, and that it is a discerner of the thoughts and intents of the heart. *When you are walking in the Word of God, you will prosper and be in health.*

We cannot settle for prosperity in the physical or the mental realm only. It would be easy just to settle for spiritual prosperity, but we can't afford to be lazy and to discount physical and mental prosperity simply because we are saved and filled with the Holy Spirit. It is the will of God for us to be made whole—spirit, soul, and body—and to be kept that way until the return of our Lord Jesus Christ (see 1 Thess. 5:23). As you walk in the light of God's Word, you will become prosperous in every area of your life.

## Spiritual and Physical Law

We must understand that there are laws governing every single thing in existence. Nothing is by accident. There are laws of the world of the spirit, and there are laws of the world of the natural.

The laws of the world of the natural govern our activities in this natural, physical world. We don't float; we walk. If the law of gravity were not in action, we would float. These physical laws can be manipulated. For instance, the law of gravity is used when flying an airplane, but it is superseded by another physical law, the law of lift. When you put the law of lift into operation, you can fly, but you must know something about the law of gravity in order to use the law of lift. You don't do away with the law of gravity; you just supersede it with a higher law. These are natural, physical laws, and they govern this natural, physical world.

We need to realize that the spiritual world and its laws are more powerful than the physical world and its laws. Spiritual law gave birth to physical law. The world and the physical forces governing it were created by the power of faith—a spiritual force. God, a Spirit, created all matter, and He created it with the force of faith. Hebrews 11:3 says, *...the worlds were framed by the word of God, so that things which are seen were not made of things which do appear.* The law of gravity would be meaningless if gravity were not a real force. It is the force of gravity which makes the law of gravity work. In the same way, spiritual law would be useless if the force of faith were not a real force; but faith *is* a real force. Faith is a spiritual force, a spiritual energy, a spiritual power. It is this force of faith which makes the laws of the spirit world function. When the force of faith is put to work, these laws of the spirit function according to the way God says they will.

Romans 8:2 says, *For the law of the Spirit of life in Christ Jesus hath made me free from the law of sin and death.* There are two functional laws in the world of the spirit. One, the law of sin and death, was put into operation by Adam when he disobeyed God in the Garden of Eden. The other, the law of the Spirit of life, was put into operation by Jesus Christ at His Resurrection. The law of the Spirit of life is the master law under which we operate as children of God. It supersedes the law of sin and death, and faith causes it to function. There are certain elements which, when combined, will bring forth the result God intends. Salvation is available to every human being on the face of the earth because the Word says that anyone who calls upon the name of the Lord shall be saved (see Joel 2:32; Rom. 10:13). This higher spiritual law of life is here in the earth, but every day people die and go to hell. Why? Because the law of salvation hasn't been put to work in their particular lives. It will work *only* when it is put to work.

This same rule is true in prosperity. There are certain laws governing prosperity revealed in God's Word. Faith causes them to function. They will work when they are put to work, and they will stop working when the force of faith is stopped.

The Bible says that God's Word is established forever, and it is law (see 1 Pet. 1:25). When God speaks, His words become law in the world of the spirit. Jesus said, *Man shall not live by bread alone, but by every word that proceedeth out of the mouth of God* (Matt. 4:4).

The success formulas in the Word of God produce results when used as directed. Mark 11:23 says, *...whosoever shall say unto this mountain, Be thou removed, and be thou* *cast into the sea; and shall not doubt in his heart, but shall believe that those things which he saith shall come to pass; he shall have whatsoever he saith.* Here Jesus introduced a principle—a spiritual law—that works. It doesn't make sense to the natural mind that with faith you can have whatever you say even though it may be contrary to what you can see with your physical eyes, but Jesus said it and by the eternal Almighty God, it is so! When you act on it, mix your faith with it, don't doubt in your heart, this spiritual law will work for you!

Do you see how this functions? The laws of prosperity work the same as the laws of salvation, healing, and so forth. We are dealing with the same God, the same Word, the same Jesus, the same force of faith, and the same thief, Satan, who is trying to steal it away from you! There are many people who have the world's idea of salvation, and they will go to hell with it! It is wrong! Man's good intentions have nothing to do with eternal salvation. You can have good intentions to fly, but you will never get off the ground until you make the proper arrangements—until you put the proper laws into operation. A farmer can intend to have a good crop, but if he never plants the seed, how can he possibly produce a harvest? These laws, both spiritual and physical, must be followed if you expect to get results.

The Bible says in Deuteronomy 29:29, *The secret things belong unto the Lord our God: but those things which are revealed belong unto us and to our children for ever, that we may do all the words of this law.* Any law that God has ever revealed to His saints will never pass away. It will work every time it is put to work. Anything God taught Abraham or his descendants about operating financially will work just as well today as it did several thousand years ago. If you don't believe it, you've never met a Jew! The formulas still work, and they always will! Every law God has given us is recorded in His Word, and He sent the Holy Spirit as our Teacher to lead and guide us in these laws and show us how they operate *for one reason* – so that we will put them to work. Each time one of these laws operates, it glorifies the Almighty God who spoke it and adds one more defeat to Satan who said it would not work.

## World's System vs. God's System

God has a highly organized system to meet the needs of every facet of your life. The world's system of meeting our needs works exactly opposite from God's system. *God's system is totally adequate.* The world's idea of anything is very limited at best and stands 99 9/10 percent chance of being totally wrong. As believers, we must be careful not to limit God in our individual lives to what the world says is so. The problem with the world and its system of operations is that there is a spiritual mad dog loose in it and his name is Satan.

The world has a system of healing that is a miserable failure! We thank God for what good has been done with it, but we are forced to admit it falls far short of being adequate to meet the needs of the sick around us. Some men are dedicated to it as if it were a god. The world's system of healing makes a god of the hospital and a god of medicine. Actually, for the most part, it leaves God out entirely, and without God, it will not work! There is no way to get healing except through the power of God, either directly by His power or by the power He built into the human body. No man on earth can heal apart from God.

There are two choices before you – the world's system of healing or God's system of healing. God's system and its laws are contradictory to the world's system. The world cannot understand God's system of caring for the human body. The Bible says the things of God are foolishness to the world (see 1 Cor. 2:14). God made the human body. He definitely should be able to repair it. Ford Motor Company has that much sense! If they can build the whole car, surely they can build parts for it.

# The Laws of Prosperity

We haven't known much about the law of the Spirit of life in Christ Jesus and a lack of understanding has caused problems in making this law function for our benefit. The apostle Paul wrote, *And be not conformed to this world: but be ye transformed by the renewing of your mind* (Rom. 12:2). In order to be successful at God's business, we must understand how His system works. Don't expect God's best to come from the world's system. He will work around and through it in order to reach you, but it is always far below His best.

The absolute priority in studying prosperity is that you should *never* think of it from a carnal viewpoint, from the world's attitude. You must train yourself to think in line with God's Word. If you're not careful, when you think of the laws of prosperity, all you will see is money—only a very small part of prosperity. *True prosperity is God manifesting Himself to us in His Word.* If He is manifesting Himself through His Word, He is always within easy contact because you can handle the Word. The only way you can have God with you on a continual daily basis is through His Word. We should not judge by our feelings or by our emotions, but by what God has said in His Word.

Let's look for a moment at the world of finance, the biggest problem area on earth. Sickness is not our main concern. There are many healthy people who are head over heels in debt, *and God's people had no business being in debt!* Here again, we find that the world has a system of finance which is complex and very poor in operation. It continually rocks back and forth between the two extremes of depression and inflation.

However, when you are functioning in God's system of finance, life can be very simple. Don't borrow from anyone—get it from God. The problem with borrowing is that it is controlled by the world's system. In order to borrow, you must subordinate yourself to another person. Proverbs 22:7 says that the borrower is the servant to the lender. By borrowing, you subordinate your name to another person. This is very important because of the spiritual significance of your name. Your name is the same as your nature. If your name is good, then you are good—your reputation is good. You can do whatever your name can do. However, when you borrow and go into debt to someone else, you bow your knee to that person and look to him as your source of supply. This creates a spiritual problem that can be very serious, particularly if the other person is ungodly.

Look to God, He will *give* to you, not loan to you! Believers need to learn how to operate in God's system. It isn't easy to learn; but as you search the Word, you will have the desire to know God's system. When you begin to operate by it and live by faith in every area of your life, God will step in and make up what you don't know. He will put you over! The deeper you get into the Word and the more you learn, the more you will expand; the more you expand, the more Satan will fight; the more he fights, the bigger the victory; the bigger your victory, the more glory to God; the more glory to God, the more you will expand! It is constant growth!

At this point, let me emphasize Satan's part in this. When you hear the Word, when you learn to believe God—especially in the area of giving—*you become dangerous to Satan!* Jesus taught that the sower sows the Word and Satan comes *immediately* to take out the Word which was sown (see Mark 4:1-20). Why? For three basic reasons:

(1) The Word of God is the key to the laws of the Spirit.
(2) The laws of the Spirit govern the laws of the natural.
(3) Satan works in the natural world.

When you take the power of these laws and function them by faith, Satan is finished! When you learn the rules of the game, he is through. He is a defeated foe!

Let me mention that these laws of prosperity will work for anyone, regardless of their age! My children operate them just as successfully as my wife and I. They have learned God's system of finance and can absolutely believe God for anything in the world and get it! I remember when we needed a van for the ministry to carry our equipment. My daughter Kellie came to me and said, "Daddy, I want to be the first to give money for this truck." She had a couple of dollars, so she gave it, and we made an agreement together. Then she started confessing the return on her money and got it! It didn't take her several months, and she didn't start whining about it—she simply said, "In the name of Jesus, it's mine!"

One day our little boy, who was about six years old at the time, came in and said, "Daddy, I want to give my money." No one had said anything to him, he just came through leadership of the Lord. He doesn't fully realize that God is directing him, he just responds to it. He's a child. (This is how we are to respond as children in obedience.) He gave his money into the ministry and began believing God for the return. A few days later, he got it! A six-year-old boy! It works for him proficiently! Why? Because he is a born-again believer filled with the Holy Spirit. He is a child of God, and he has a right to work these laws. It isn't a man's age that causes the law of gravity to work; the law of gravity works because gravity is a force. Remember, faith is a spiritual force and works by spiritual law (see Rom. 3:27).

## Prosperity: The World vs. God

Once again, we have the world's information opposing God's information. If you know what God thinks or what He has said, then you have a very easy task of thinking and believing the same way. If you know what God has said, you cannot be deceived.

To the world, prosperity, like everything else, is completely born of the senses, or the sense-ruled mind. The world is governed by natural impulse and the physical senses. Its slogan is *seeing is believing.* If you can see it, taste it, hear it, smell it, or feel it, then it must be true; if you can't contact it with your physical senses, it is not true.

As we have discussed earlier in this chapter, the world's definition of prosperity is very limited in its scope — financial ability and power. In fact, it goes only this far by its own admission. The world itself admits that it has no power to overcome poverty, sickness, spiritual ills, or social ills.

*True prosperity is the ability to use God's power to meet the needs of mankind in any realm of life.* This covers much more than just finances, politics, and society. Money is not the only degree of prosperity. You can have all the money in the world and still be poverty-stricken spiritually, mentally, and physically. Money is the lowest form of power that exists on earth. Do you know what is the highest? *The power of prayer!* You can pray in the name of Jesus, and God will use His ability to handle your situation, whatever it is. It takes the power of God to make you completely whole. God's power is the only power that covers the entire spectrum of human existence. God is more than enough!

To live a prosperous life, your soul must prosper in *all* the truth of the Word. God's power is in direct relationship with His Word. He has used His Word to release His power. He has sent His Word to us so that we may be in contact with His great power. Isaiah was quoting God Himself when he wrote, *So shall my word be that goeth forth out of my mouth: it shall not return unto me void, but it shall accomplish that which I please, and it shall prosper in the thing whereto I sent it* (Is. 55:11). His power covers the entire spectrum of human existence — so also then does His Word. We can see it in scriptures such as Hebrews 1:3 that says He is upholding ALL things by the power of His Word and Hebrews 4:12,13 that the Word is a living thing which covers spirit, soul, body, and thought-life. It even goes so far as to say that *nothing* in the earth is hidden from the Word of God.

Your faith is in direct relation to the level of the Word in you. Get your Word-level up so that you can believe spiritually, mentally, physically, financially, and socially. Thus you will be in the position to handle any problem that comes your way according to the Word of God. *You* may not have the answer, but God has! Getting through to you is His only difficulty! God always knows the answer, but we are not always in a position to hear what He is saying.

If you know how to use God's ability to receive healing and never use it to help anyone but yourself, then it won't work for you very long. If you can believe God for healing, help someone else get healed. Spread it around! If you know how to believe God financially, start helping the people around you. You will begin to grow as you reach out to others.

In John 14:18-23, Jesus was teaching His disciples and gave the perfect outline of prosperity: *I will not leave you comfortless: I will come to you. Yet a little while, and the world seeth me no more; but ye see me: because I live, ye shall live also. At that day ye shall know that I am in my Father, and ye in me, and I in you. He that hath my commandments, and keepeth them, he it is that loveth me: and he that loveth me shall be loved of my Father, and **I will love him, and will manifest myself to him.** Judas saith unto him, not Iscariot, Lord, how is it that thou wilt manifest thyself unto us, and not unto the world? Jesus answered and said unto him, If a man love me, he will keep my words: and my Father will love him, and **we will come unto him, and make our abode with him.***

This is speaking of a manifestation of God. When God manifests Himself to you and lives with you, then you are living in prosperity. You see, God by the Holy Spirit is here in the world. He is ready to move whenever a sinner makes Jesus the Lord of his life, but He will not manifest

Himself in a person's life until that person calls on Him. If God's presence were enough, every human being on earth would get saved because we all are in the presence of the Holy Spirit. He was sent to earth on the day of Pentecost and is still here today. The manifestation of God is the important thing. When we operate in the Word of God, when we keep His Word, then Jesus will manifest Himself, or make Himself real, to us. He won't just be there—He will live there! Do you see the difference? If we put His Word first in our lives, Jesus will reveal Himself to us. Then whenever a problem arises in the physical realm, we know the answer is in His Word. We also know the Great One *living* in us will put us over when we act on that Word, no matter how impossible the situation is.

Some people are waiting for a special manifestation of God's grace before they will get saved, but they don't have to wait at all. We are born of His Word (see 1 Pet. 1:23). If a man will confess Jesus as Lord and believe that God has raised Him from the dead, he will be saved (see Rom. 10:9,10). It is a simple matter of believing God's Word. You don't have to wait to receive salvation—it is being offered. You don't have to wait to receive prosperity—it is being offered. These things are offered by Jesus in His Word.

You know, the Bible says in Philippians 4:19 that God will meet your needs *according to his riches in glory by Christ Jesus,* not according to your need. I have heard it preached that if you ask God for one hundred dollars but need only twenty dollars, you'll probably just get ten dollars. You won't find that in the Bible, but God does say:

*If ye be willing and obedient, ye shall eat the good of the land* (Is. 1:19).

*What things soever ye desire, when ye pray, believe that ye receive them, and ye shall have them* (Mark 11:24).

*...ye have not, because ye ask not* (James 4:2).

When you act on the Word of God, the desires of your heart will begin to grow and line up with God. Then He

24

can cause *all* grace to abound toward you (see 2 Cor. 9:8). The first step is to get your mind off of yourself. Begin to take up the needs of the Body of Christ as if they were your own. The Word states very plainly that if a man comes to you needing food and clothes, don't just pray for him and send him away cold and hungry. Feed him and clothe him!

Another thing, God will not just meet your needs *according to your job.* Businessmen have come to me and said that these things work for me only because I am a preacher, but this is foolishness! I know preachers everywhere it's not working for. Some men say, "But I don't have the opportunity for people to give to me. I'm not out preaching. They don't think of me when they give. I have to work for mine." Well, if you have more faith in your job and your own ability to work than you have in the Word of God, then it definitely won't work for you. God will certainly use what is available in your job to bless you or even get you a better one, but He is not limited to your job unless *you* limit Him to it. If you will stop and think for a moment, God did not make His covenant with a preacher; He made it with a farmer, a working man named Abram. The Scriptures show that Abram turned to the Sodomite king and said, "I don't even want the string from your sandal because you could say a man made Abram rich" (see Gen. 14:23). No man made Abraham rich. God made him rich. Can you see this?

There is a basic, fundamental truth that runs throughout the entire Bible, throughout God's history of dealing with man. Every time there was a need, no matter what that need was, God had a man somewhere who had the resources—spiritually, mentally, or financially—to meet that need. For Israel, there was Moses. For the world, there was Jesus. For Jesus, there was a man with a donkey. For Ephesus, there was Paul. The Bible says God gave gifts to men—apostles, prophets, evangelists, pastors, teachers (see Eph. 4:11). He had a man to provide every need. No one person will ever be so spiritual that he doesn't need other people. We all need one another.

Begin to include the Body of Christ in your needs. Begin to include the lost in your needs. If a man came to you needing clothes and you didn't have any clothes to give him, both of you would be in trouble. You need clothes for yourself, and you need to be able to supply him with clothes. Jesus said, "Why do you worry about what you will eat and what you will wear? Your heavenly Father knows you have need of these things" (see Matt. 6:31,32). But He also said, *Give, and it shall be given unto you; good measure, pressed down, and shaken together, and running over, shall men give into your bosom* (Luke 6:38).

When I realized this and began to consider the needs of others before my own, I found that my needs were met supernaturally! It was uncanny! I had spent practically all of my adult life in debt. It seemed that every business venture I tried just fell apart, leaving me even further in debt. Then I turned to the Lord, determined to commit myself to His Word, and began walking my bedroom floor with my Bible in my fist, shouting at the top of my voice, "My God meets all my needs according to His riches in glory by Christ Jesus!" I just kept confessing this hour after hour, day after day! My situation looked absolutely impossible at the time! I had no place to preach and nothing much to say! (One thing I *could* say was, "My God meets all my needs according to His riches in glory by Christ Jesus!" I knew that sentence very well!) Eleven months later I was completely out of debt. In the meantime, I learned to include other people in my needs by giving to them and getting involved with them. When I began to give, I suddenly realized one day how very busy I was with God's work. Years have come and gone and I haven't caught up yet. When you do this, God will move heaven and earth if necessary to reach you.

Now, a big question in the minds of many Christians is *does Satan bless people financially?* Many times it looks as though the ungodly men have all the money, but this is not true. There is more wealth hidden away than they will ever possess. The Bible says plainly that God will cause us to have the hidden wealth of the world, the hidden riches of the secret places (see Is. 45:3). The Word tells us that *the wealth of the sinner is laid up for the just* (Prov. 13:22). Why then does the sinner have it? Because there are certain facts of financial law that will work when put to work. Israel has proven this. God taught Abraham certain things that the Jews are using today, and they are still working. You won't find a Jew who believes in poverty because poverty is not in the Old Covenant. It is in religion, not in the Bible. It was put into Christianity as a religion during the Dark Ages when the Word was taken from the people and put away in monasteries. Poverty oaths were fed into Christianity when the religious hierarchy took over. The men operating it were not born-again men.

You can look at the world's system of finance and see a perfect picture of Satan's whole pattern. It can be stated in just a few words—*The thief cometh not, but for to steal, and to kill, and to destroy* (John 10:10).

How do you kill a body of water? Stop it from flowing.

How do you kill a physical body? Stop it from functioning.

How do you kill the Body of Christ financially? Pile up all the money in reservoirs and stop it from moving. Satan is a deceiver. Absolutely nothing he does is a blessing. Proverbs 1:32 confirms this, *The prosperity of fools shall destroy them.* It may look as if he is blessing, but he always destroys. He always presents a dead end, no way out. In fact, if you want to discern between the work of God and the work of Satan, remember: Satan always tells you there is no way out, but Jesus says, *I am the way* (John 14:6). If it is doubt, defeat, or discouragement, it is from Satan—ALWAYS.

By believing God and including the needs of the Body of Christ in your needs, you become an open channel for the things of God to flow through to others. Everything you have received from God flowed through Jesus. Did

Jesus ever lose anything by giving it to you? No, He still owns it all. First John 4:17 makes a startling statement, *...as he is, so are we in this world.* This does not say **as He was** or **as we are someday going to be;** it says *as he is, so are we.* In His position at the right hand of God, Jesus has more than enough to give. Well, we are His joint-heirs, and He is ready to see to it that we have enough to give (see Phil. 4:10-19).

An example of this channel can be seen in the Book of Revelation. God gave His revelation to Jesus, who signified it to His servant John by His angel; the angel gave it to John; John was to give it to the churches; and they, in turn, would give it to the Body of Christ who would feed it to the world. A constant channel, a constant flowing—the flow of love...the flow of power...the flow of money...the flow of food...the flow of everything you need!

The basic principle God has planned to use in supplying the Body of Christ and allowing the Body of Christ to supply the world is summed up in one verse from Ecclesiastes, *Cast thy bread upon the waters: for thou shalt find it after many days* (Eccl. 11:1). Give, and after a while it will come back to you again. You have to start "casting your bread" sometime—tomorrow will never do. You can't wait until your bread comes back before you cast it out. Many are waiting for their ship to come in who have never sent one out! Things don't work that way. It would be like saying to a stove, "Give me some heat, and then I'll put in some wood." You give—*then* it will be given to you again. The key is to give continually. As you are walking in the Word and God's prosperity is being produced in your life, you will reach a point when your bread is coming back to you on every wave! It is *your* job to put it on the water. It is *God's* job to see that it comes back! You do your job and let God do His, then you will be continually receiving. The more you give, the more you will get; the more you get, the more you will have to give. God intended for these things to work this way. When you get to this point, more will be coming in than you can give away!

Satan operates in a way exactly opposite from this. Everything he does spells filth and stoppage. When you see a wicked man with a great amount of wealth, you are looking at a financial reservoir created by Satan to stop the flow. *And Jesus looked around and said to His disciples, With what difficulty will those who possess wealth and keep on holding it enter the kingdom of God!* (Mark 10:23, *Amplified*). If a man has a million dollars in a safe and won't spend it, it is absolutely worthless—to him and to everyone around him. There are many people who could benefit from it, but he has the channel blocked. The only one profiting from this kind of thing is Satan. He uses the forces of hate, fear, and greed to keep financial resources locked up. Proverbs 1:19 tells us that greed takes away the life of its possessors. Satan can show you how to *make* money, but he can't show you how to *keep* it. Selfishness is *never* able to maintain what it builds—it *always* destroys.

Suppose a man decided to save his left arm and just use his right one, thinking that years later when his right arm got tired, he could switch over and use the left one again. What would happen to his left arm? It would lose its ability to function, wouldn't it? Now, this is a foolish idea, but the principle is true for a man with one hundred thousand dollars stashed away because of fear that one of these days there wouldn't be any money left.

If you are exercising this kind of fear with a few dollars, you are just as guilty of being a reservoir—a dead end, a satanic stoppage—as the man who stopped up a million dollars. Someone with no more than a secondhand shirt can be just as guilty of greed as a man with millions of dollars piled up somewhere. One is just as deceived as the other. To a person who is cold, a secondhand shirt looks pretty good. As I pointed out before, the Bible does not say that money is the root of all evil; it says *the love of money* is the root of all evil (1 Tim. 6:10), and there are millions of people committing that sin who don't have a dime! God can do more with fifteen cents given in faith than kings can do with mountains of gold! The little widow proved this with her two mites (see Mark 12:41-44). Remember not to limit God to only what you can see and understand with your head. When the entire world is completely destitute, God will still have plenty and can make it abound toward you. **As He is, so are we in this world.** So don't be afraid to become a cheerful, free-hearted giver.

In the spiritual realm as a born-again believer, you have Life and the ability to share it with others. You need to learn how to give this Life to meet their needs. The Word of God says, *How beautiful are the feet of them that preach the gospel of peace, and bring glad tidings of good things!* (Rom. 10:15). I wondered what this really meant until I heard the story of a missionary and his family who were captured by the Japanese during World War II. After they were taken captive, they were told that Washington, D.C., had fallen, that the United States had surrendered, and that Japan was in control. Well, you can imagine what this did to those people. They felt absolutely hopeless! The Japanese dragged them around the country and finally began killing them because there wasn't enough food. They took this missionary's little girl and shot her. The next day they heard a deafening roar and saw the sky covered with B-29's! Those people just went crazy! They had been completely without hope, laboring under the lie that their country was defeated. Later a G.I. kicked in the door on their compound and said, "You're free," and when he did, the missionary fell down before him and kissed his boots! You have the life-giving force of God Himself residing inside you, and the world is desperate for that life! Don't be stingy with it. Freely you have received…freely give.

When you make it your need to get salvation into the hands of the people, when you make it your purpose to feed the gospel to the unsaved, God will support what you do. This is true prosperity! God has obligated Himself to communicate the message of Jesus Christ to the world. He will move heaven and earth to do it because, to the man who has never heard it, Jesus has never died or been resurrected from the dead. To that man, the sacrifice of Jesus means nothing. The Word says in 1 John 4:17, *...as he is, so are we in this world.* God is feeding us through Jesus. When you go to the Lord, He has more than enough to meet the need. Have you ever turned to the Lord with a problem and had Him say, "Well, that's new! You've come up with something heaven can't cover"? Of course not! God has more than enough to solve the worst problem you could have. Jesus is the channel to us, and we are the channel to the world.

True prosperity is the ability to look a man in the eye in his moment of impossibility and take his needs as your own. Those who are spiritual are to help those who are not. We are to bear one another's burdens. When a brother comes to you with a problem, join with him in prayer, join your faith with his. Put pressure on Satan with the name of Jesus and get him off the man. Put pressure on the laws of the Spirit of life in Christ Jesus. Lean on your righteousness in Jesus Christ. Lean *hard* on it! Lean *hard* on your sonship. Lean *hard* on the Blood of Jesus. Praise God, they work!

# Chapter Two
## *The Established Covenant and the Established Heart*

God has established His covenant in the earth. *Everything He does is determined by this covenant.* Jesus of Nazareth was born into this world, died on the cross, went to hell, paid the sin price, and was raised from the dead because of the covenant God made with man. God does not show partiality by choosing certain people to save or to heal; His blessings are for *all* the people who meet the conditions of the covenant (see 1 Pet. 2:24).

God has established His covenant—for salvation, for healing, for deliverance, for prosperity—and these provisions of the covenant are set out in God's Word. His Word is His covenant, His bond. When you consider a person's word, you think of his integrity: *Will he do what he says? Is his word good? Is his name good?* A person's name is judged as good or bad by whether or not he keeps his word. Your name doesn't make your word good. Your word makes your name good. Herein lies the power in the name of Jesus; His name is good because His Word is good. God has magnified His Word even above His name (see Ps. 138:2).

God's covenant has been established in the earth. Now man must establish his heart in God's covenant. It is the combination of the established covenant of God and your established heart in this covenant that produces results. If your heart is not established in the covenant, then the covenant will never mean anything to you. Ephesians 2:12 says, *That at that time ye were without Christ, being aliens from the commonwealth of Israel, and strangers from the covenants of promise, having no hope, and without God in the world.*

Being without God is spiritual bankruptcy. It doesn't matter what God has done—if you don't know about it or can't get in it, you are spiritually bankrupt. Eventually, you will become physically bankrupt in one form or another. You will have nowhere to turn. You can't depend on your physical capabilities because your flesh just isn't enough to get you through. Certainly, this is true of your mind, your mental capabilities. Men with the strongest minds in the world are committing suicide at an alarming rate!

A man without God in the world is a man without a covenant. He has nothing to believe. He has nothing to rely on. There are many Christians who actually do not know *what* to believe. They say, "How does this work? I'm trying my best to believe God, but I just can't seem to do it!" There are many fine, upstanding people—born again, filled with the Spirit of God—who are absolutely defeated in every area of their lives (physically, mentally, socially, and financially). Why? Because they don't know the covenant. If they don't know what God has said, there is no way He can reach them.

Someone might say, "I'm going to believe God." Well, what about Him are you going to believe...that He is God? This is fine, but it won't go very far. You must find out what the covenant says God has agreed to do. A businessman has that much sense. When two people enter into partnership together, they must know what to believe. If they don't, they will get into a misunderstanding. Both of them can be completely honest and still destroy the partnership simply because they do not understand each other and do not know what to expect from one another. To avoid this, they must come together, decide the terms of their partnership, and write them down. When they make this agreement (or covenant) together, they know what to expect from each other.

You as a believer have God's covenant, God's Word. It is available to you. However, if you don't put it to use, you are on the same level as the man who does not know salvation is for him. He is hell-bound. You are poverty-bound or bound in some other area where the Word gives you freedom. If you do not use the covenant, you will live in defeat. This was true in my life. I was born again and filled with the Holy Spirit but lived almost four years in total defeat as a Christian, particularly in the area of finances. I was trying my best to believe God. My intentions were good, but I had no idea of what was available to me and no knowledge of what God had provided in Jesus Christ. Satan kept me behind the eight ball continually! You see, a man can have a million dollars in the bank, but if he can't write a check, he is as destitute as the next guy!

A good illustration of this is the man who saved his money to come to America. He scrimped and saved and finally got the money for a boat ticket with just enough left to buy a box of crackers and some cheese. He rationed it to provide a little each day until the boat landed. During the voyage, he would look into the dining room where everyone was eating and then go back to his room and eat his little food ration. When the boat was anchoring in New York Harbor, a steward stopped him and said, "Sir, I've noticed that you haven't eaten a meal throughout this trip. Is our service offensive to you? Is the food unsatisfactory?" The man answered, "Oh, no! I'm not offended. It's just that I only had the money for my ticket. There wasn't enough left over for meals." Then the steward said, "Well, sir, the meals were included in the ticket!" You see, those meals were his, but he didn't know it! His ticket was an agreement. It belonged to him, but he didn't know the terms of that agreement! He had as much right to those meals as the captain of the ship, but he settled for crackers and cheese instead. Most Christians have been "eating crackers and cheese" by not knowing their covenant with God, by not knowing what is already theirs through Jesus Christ.

## The Established Covenant

Abraham...Moses...David...Solomon...why did God bless these men? Why have so few men found the blessings of God in finance? We need to renew our minds to God's reason for financial blessings. In the Book of Deuteronomy, we see the predominant rule to remember in living a prosperous life: *And thou say in thine heart, My power and the might of mine hand hath gotten me this wealth. But thou shalt remember the Lord thy God: for it is he that giveth thee power to get wealth, that he may establish his covenant which he sware unto thy fathers, as it is this day* (Deut. 8:17,18).

The predominant rule: *God gives the power to get wealth.* Why? *To establish His covenant.*

Let's read further from Deuteronomy 9:5,6: *Not for thy righteousness, or for the uprightness of thine heart, dost thou go to possess their land: but for the wickedness of these nations the Lord thy God doth drive them out from before thee, and that he may perform the word which the Lord sware unto thy fathers, Abraham, Isaac, and Jacob. Understand therefore, that the Lord thy God giveth thee not this good land to possess it for thy righteousness; for thou art a stiffnecked people.* In other words, Moses was saying, "God didn't drive those people from their land because of *your* righteousness. He did it because He promised to do it. He had made an agreement with Abraham, Isaac, and Jacob." Now the people did everything they possibly could to keep Him from it. They broke the covenant in every way, but God instituted the priesthood to offer sacrifices for their sins. They had no righteousness to rely on, so God gave them a way out. He went to great lengths to establish the covenant even among unrighteous people!

Deuteronomy 29:9 says, *Keep therefore the words of this covenant, and do them, that ye may prosper in all that ye do.* According to this, we should be prosperous in *everything* we do, *but we must keep the words of the covenant.*

## The Established Covenant and the Established Heart

God gave instruction along these same lines to Joshua during the most critical situation in his life. Moses was dead and Joshua was to take over leadership of Israel in his place, a very difficult job to do. Moses...the man who talked with God face-to-face...the man who produced water from a rock in the middle of the desert. Moses walked in prosperity! When he needed water, God gave him the ability to get it. The power of God brought the water, and it was priceless! This is real prosperity!

Now I want you to realize the uniqueness of Joshua's situation. This is the moment when both the natural world and the spiritual world are hanging in the balance. These are God's people; if they fail, there will be no Jesus! If God fails them, there will be no redemption! God must keep His covenant alive in the earth in order to bring forth Jesus, the Redeemer. He had to have a man who would listen to Him.

At this critical time in history, where does God put the exclamation point? What does He deem important? He speaks to Joshua and says, *There shall not any man be able to stand before thee all the days of thy life: as I was with Moses, so I will be with thee: I will not fail thee, nor forsake thee. Be strong and of a good courage: for unto this people shalt thou divide for an inheritance the land, which I sware unto their fathers to give them. Only be thou strong and very courageous, that thou mayest observe to do according to all the law, which Moses my servant commanded thee: turn not from it to the right hand or to the left, that thou mayest prosper whithersoever thou goest. This book of the law shall not depart out of thy mouth; but thou shalt meditate therein day and night, that thou mayest observe to do according to all that is written therein: for then thou shalt make thy way prosperous, and then thou shalt have good success...be not afraid, neither be thou dismayed: for the Lord thy God is with thee withersoever thou goest* (Josh. 1:5-9).

In verse five, we see the key to wealth and prosperity once again: *I will be with thee: I will not fail thee, nor forsake thee.* Here is God manifesting Himself to man! Jesus said the same thing in Matthew 28:20, *Lo, I am with you alway, even unto the end of the world.* He said in John 14:16 that He would send the Holy Spirit as our Comforter to abide with us forever. Prosperity is a by-product of God walking with us and manifesting Himself to us.

God could have told Joshua many things—to fast so many days each week or to pray so many hours each day. He could have said, "If you'll believe Me, I'll do great miracles," or "If you'll believe Me, there will be a cloud by day and a pillar of fire by night." He could have said, "You'll not have to worry when you come to another Red Sea or when your enemies come against you." But He didn't say anything of the kind. At this important hour in Joshua's life—at this vital time in the plan of redemption—God said, *This book of the law shall not depart out of thy mouth; but thou shalt meditate therein day and night, that thou mayest observe to do according to all that is written therein: for then thou shalt make thy way prosperous, and then thou shalt have good success.* Another translation says, *You shall deal wisely in all the affairs of life.*

What did God put first? Meditation in His Word.

With one word of His mouth, He established Psalm 138:2 that says He has magnified His Word even above His name. You see, when you put the Word of God first in your life and it becomes your final authority, prosperity is the result. It is inevitable because the Word of God covers every situation in life. THE WORD IS FINAL AUTHORITY.

All these words God spoke to Joshua would have been useless if he had disobeyed and not meditated in the Word day and night. Only by meditation in the Word will you be able to see how to do what is written there. Proverbs 23:7 tells us that as a man thinks in his heart, so is he. Learn to take the Word of God and meditate in it. Then when the world says, "There's no way out," you can just smile and say, "Oh yes, there is a way. His name is Jesus."

God said, *If you will meditate in My Word, you will prosper and have good success.* In other words, you will deal wisely in *all* the affairs of life. If you do this, prosperity will be no problem. It doesn't matter who you are or what situation you are in, if you can deal wisely in all the affairs of your life, you will triumph. Paul and Silas proved this when they were in jail. They praised God at midnight, and evidently they dealt wisely in that affair because the prison doors popped open!

A good businessman knows that making money is not his biggest problem. Anyone can make money if he knows how to deal wisely. He can take fifty cents and turn it into a fortune if he knows exactly what to do with it. If you knew exactly how to deal wisely with the money in your purse or billfold—if you knew what to do, where to go, whom to talk with, and what to say—success would be inevitable.

The truly successful man is one who knows the Lord, has learned to believe God, and can share it with others. This man is valuable to God, to himself, to the people around him, and he is dangerous to Satan.

Remember, it is God who gives the power to get wealth in order that His covenant may be established. God and His Word are one. **When you are in the presence of the Word of God, you are in the presence of God Himself.** John 1:1 says, *In the beginning was the Word, and the Word was with God, and the Word was God.* There is no way that you can have God manifested in your life without His Word. Now there are special manifestations of God's grace, but the Christian is not supposed to live on these. We are to live in a constant manifestation of God's presence from His Word. You keep His Word, and He will manifest Himself to you. Nothing thrills me more than to know that if I wake up in the middle of the night with some problem, all I have to do is reach for my Bible. This is the manifestation of the power of God. It will work every time for anybody who will use it! When you realize that this manifestation of God is available all the time and begin to walk in the light of it, you will become prosperous.

We have seen from the Word that God has established His covenant in the earth, but what about the New Covenant? The Word says it is a covenant of righteousness based on better promises. As we have read in Deuteronomy, God called Israel stiffnecked and unrighteous. According to the New Covenant, we have been made the righteousness of God in Jesus Christ. God does not see us as a stiffnecked people. (He sees us many times as an untaught people because we do not know the covenant, but we are not stiffnecked and unrighteous.) He sees us through the Blood of the Lamb: spotless, blameless, beyond reproach. Israel was the servant of God; we are the sons of God (see Gal. 4:7). We need to realize our rights as His children and citizens of the kingdom of God.

To illustrate, let's look at the parable of the prodigal son from Luke 15. For many years we have read this story without realizing its full significance, and it has a very important application in the area of prosperity which has been entirely overlooked. As we have read about the prodigal son coming home, we've stopped there. Our minds have been on him, but what about the other son? The prodigal son took his inheritance and squandered it. When he returned home, his father killed the fatted calf and threw a big party welcoming him with open arms. Then the other son came in, saw what had happened, and got mad at his father. He said, "I have stayed here with you, and you have never even given me a little goat. Yet when he goes off and wastes his money, you celebrate by killing a calf for him!" Then his father said, "But, son, everything I have belongs to you." In other words, he was saying, "You could have had a fatted calf anytime you wanted it. It belongs to you. I'm pleased that your brother has come home, but *you* could have had it for the asking!" You see, the other son would have settled for a goat when the calf was his all the time! The inheritance belonged to both sons; only one took advantage of it. The older son did without because of the littleness of his thinking. Most

Christians are cheating themselves out of their full inheritance in Jesus Christ because of the littleness of their thinking. By not knowing their covenant, they do not know their rights as children of Almighty God!

## Poverty vs. Prosperity

In chapter 28 of Deuteronomy, we see the blessings that come from obeying the Word of God. For instance, verses 11,12 state, *And the Lord shall make thee plenteous in goods, in the fruit of thy body, and in the fruit of thy cattle, and in the fruit of thy ground, in the land which the Lord sware unto thy fathers to give thee. The Lord shall open unto thee his good treasure.* You see, God blessed Abraham and his descendants with prosperity because He swore it in the covenant. Praise God!

Then beginning with verse 15, we find an outline of the curse of the law. *But it shall come to pass, if thou wilt not hearken unto the voice of the Lord thy God, to observe to do all his commandments and his statutes...that all these curses shall come upon thee, and overtake thee.* This curse spells complete and total poverty in every area of life. **Poverty is not a blessing of God.** To believe that it is, that it carries with it some sort of humility, is to believe that God is the author of the curse, and He is not! God is the Author of the blessing.

God did not curse Adam; He built a garden for him and provided everything he could possibly ever need or want. Satan is the one who brought in the curse. When Adam united with Satan, everything in the earth was cursed. Then the covenant God made with Abraham provided an umbrella—a protection, an avenue of escape from this curse. As long as Abraham walked with the Lord and listened to His Word, he was protected; but the moment he disregarded the voice of the Lord, relying on his own understanding, he would step from under this protective umbrella and become vulnerable to Satan once again.

Why does it seem so difficult to get along with God? He knows the difference between right and wrong and the foundation laws upon which these values are constructed. He has understanding and wisdom about the laws governing life. He established His system to work a certain way, then Satan deceived us into believing that the opposite was true. God is not being disagreeable with us. He is refusing to agree with Satan. This happened with Eve in the Garden of Eden. God had said, "If you eat the fruit, you will surely die." Then Satan came along and convinced her that it wasn't true by saying, "Can it really be that God has said...?" He convinced her that God's Word was not true, so she disobeyed God and Adam followed her. The law functioned and at that very moment they died spiritually. Physical death was to follow years later.

From the time of Adam's fall, man was cursed. Through the years he was trained under deception and did not have the necessary spiritual knowledge and understanding to escape it. After several generations had passed, Adam's teachings to his own sons had been forgotten, and no one knew anything about God or about spiritual law. Most of the things God had said were absolutely foreign to the human mind. Jesus said, "Give, and it shall be given to you again," but this is contrary to our thinking. We say, "That's stupid! It doesn't make sense...anybody knows that if you give it away, you won't have it anymore!" But God knows the foundation principle of the law of giving. Satan knows it too, but he will try to deceive you in order to keep you ignorant, weak, and powerless so that he can govern you.

When God made His covenant with Abraham, most people could not understand. As long as they obeyed God, they were blessed. However, when they relied on their own understanding, they would go back under the curse again. God was telling them, "If you won't follow My Word and do what I tell you, there is nothing I can do for you. I cannot usurp authority over your own free will."

The Established Covenant and the Established Heart

Let's stop and consider for a moment that when God made His covenant with Abraham, Isaac, and Jacob, He promised to take care of them and their descendants. **They were free men!** Consequently, every Jewish slave who bore the lash under Egyptian rule was a free man! There was only one problem...they didn't know it! Therefore, God called Moses and gave him the ability and authority to write down the covenant God had made with Abraham. This way, the people would know what had been done and what had been agreed to. Moses went forth in the name of the covenant, performed miracles by the power of God in the face of Pharaoh, and led God's people out of bondage. They could have gone free 400 years before, but they didn't know their covenant! God has laid out His innermost thoughts and desires, His perfect will, in the form of a contract and placed them in the Bible. They are available to set us free from Satan's authority, by the Spirit of God in the name of Jesus. Jesus said, *If ye continue in my word, then are ye my disciples indeed; And ye shall know the truth, and the truth shall make you free* (John 8:31,32).

We have seen from the Word that the covenant of God has been established. We have seen that prosperity is a blessing of Abraham and that poverty is under the curse of the law. How does this affect us as members of the Body of Christ under the New Covenant?

Galatians 3:13,14,29 says, *Christ hath redeemed us from the curse of the law, being made a curse for us: for it is written, Cursed is every one that hangeth on a tree: That the blessing of Abraham might come on the Gentiles through Jesus Christ; that we might receive the promise of the Spirit through faith. And if ye be Christ's, then are ye Abraham's seed, and heirs according to the promise.*

Jesus bore the curse of the law in our behalf. He beat Satan and took away his power. Consequently, there is no reason for you to live under the curse of the law, no reason for you to live in poverty of any kind. Many born-again believers live in spiritual poverty, spiritual malnutrition. They are mighty, spiritual supermen in the embryo but not growing an ounce because they are not being properly fed. **Spiritual growth comes only by feeding and acting on the Word of God.** *Desire the sincere milk of the word, that ye may grow thereby* (1 Pet. 2:2).

Since God's covenant has been established and prosperity is a provision of this covenant, you need to realize that prosperity belongs to you *now!* Someone might say, "God can see into the future. He knows that if I had money, I would spend it unwisely or act ugly with it. That's why I don't have any." Well, you are probably right! The fact that you have more faith in this than you have in the Word of God and in your own competence as a Christian is keeping you robbed. Satan sold you that lie, not God. You *must* realize that it is God's will for you to prosper (see 3 John 2). This is available to you, and frankly, it would be stupid of you not to partake of it! When a man realizes that prosperity belongs to him, takes the Word of God, becomes prosperous, and then gives it away, he is valuable. The apostle Paul learned the spiritual law of giving and operated it proficiently. He was strong enough in the Lord to believe for prosperity, receive it, then give it away. This is a valuable sacrifice; it really means something.

The Word of God says, "Give, and it shall be given unto you again." As you begin to operate this law, you will see that you can't get rid of it! As you give, it will be returned to you faster than you can keep giving it away! As we read in Deuteronomy 8:18, God gives us the power to get wealth in order to establish His covenant. He does it because He said He would! When you fully realize that you have Him and He has you, that you can do *all* things through Christ who strengthens you (see Phil. 4:13), all the pride in your heart melts and you know that without Him you can do nothing. As you begin to understand these things, you won't be afraid to give. You won't be afraid to turn loose of it. When you give, you will receive and have even more to give, a constant flowing! Praise the Lord!

## The Established Heart

God has established His covenant in the earth, but it is not enough just to know this. For the covenant to be of any value, we must have our hearts established in it. Psalm 112 is a perfect description of the established heart. It describes the prosperous man and gives insight into his prosperity. Let's examine it closely.

*Praise ye the Lord. Blessed is the man that feareth the Lord, that delighteth greatly in his commandments.* What type of man is blessed of God? The man who fears the Lord and delights greatly in His commandments, in the established covenant of God.

*His seed shall be mighty upon earth: the generation of the upright shall be blessed. Wealth and riches shall be in his house:* **and his righteousness endureth for ever.** No one can take it away! When God gives you something, you should have no fear of losing it. God has given you His Word. You can stand firmly on it because it belongs to you!

*Unto the upright there ariseth light in the darkness: he is gracious, and full of compassion, and righteous. A good man sheweth favour, and lendeth: he will guide his affairs with discretion* [or good judgment]. *Surely he shall not be moved for ever: the righteous shall be in everlasting remembrance. He shall not be afraid of evil tidings: his heart is fixed, trusting in the Lord. His heart is established.* God has established His covenant, and this man has established his heart in the covenant. **His heart is fixed, trusting in the Lord.** You can't scare him with bad tidings about the fuel shortage, high interest rates, or anything else. He trusts completely and totally in the Lord and gets what he needs by his covenant with God. When you are established and operating in the covenant of God, Satan can't corner you.

**You must realize that prosperity is the will of God for you.** Knowledge of His will brings results. Once you know for sure that something is God's will, you should not be without it any longer. If you do not know that healing belongs to you, you will hesitate, wondering if it is God's will and never establish it in your own life. You will never really believe it for yourself. Many people have been healed through the prayers of other believers and still have difficulty with their health even after God has healed them a dozen times. However, once they see in the Word that healing belongs to them, that Jesus bought and paid for it at Calvary, that He bore the stripes, then they will not accept sickness again. Why? Because the Word becomes established in their hearts and a force rises up within them—the force of faith. This is also true in prosperity. Poverty is under the curse of the law, and Jesus Christ has redeemed us from the curse and has established us in abundance, not bare necessity!

Stop and think for a moment. What is **your** heart established in? Sin or righteousness? Death or abundant life? Sickness and disease or healing and divine health? Poverty or prosperity? Faith or fear?

The only way you will establish your heart so that it is absolutely fixed—concrete and immovable, trusting in the Lord—is by the Word of God. Go to the Word and feed on it: read it, study it, meditate in it. Then your heart will be established, fixed, trusting in the Lord, and Psalm 112 will be a description of your life in Christ Jesus.

## The Wisdom of God

The established heart comes by meditation in the Word of God. We have seen from the Book of Joshua that if a person will meditate in the Word day and night and do all that is written therein, he will prosper and deal wisely in his affairs. It is through this kind of meditation in the Word that you will discover what God has to say about finances.

Proverbs 3:13,14 says, *Happy is the man that findeth wisdom, and the man that getteth understanding. For the merchandise of it is better than the merchandise of silver, and the gain thereof than fine gold.* In other words, there is a better market for wisdom and understanding than for gold and silver. The merchandise of it is greater; it will provide more. Solomon proved this. People from faraway countries heard about the wisdom of Solomon and brought him wealth and riches because of it.

Verses 15,16, *She* [Wisdom] *is more precious than rubies: and all the things thou canst desire are not to be compared unto her. Length of days is in her right hand; and in her left hand riches and honour.* **Wisdom actually possesses riches and honor.** Does Wisdom belong to us? Again, we go to the established covenant for the answer. Let's see what the Word has to say about it.

First Corinthians 1:30 states very plainly that Jesus has been made unto us wisdom. James 1:5,6 says, *If any of you lack wisdom, let him ask of God, that giveth to all men liberally, and upbraideth not; and it shall be given him. But let him ask in faith, nothing wavering.* Paul prayed in Colossians 1:9,10 *that ye might be filled with the knowledge of his will in **all wisdom** and spiritual understanding; That ye might walk worthy of the Lord unto all pleasing, being fruitful in every good work.* We should bear fruit and succeed in every endeavor, and the Wisdom of God enables us to do this.

Now, I take for granted that you understand the importance of prayer in all these areas. Spend time before God and in His Word. Let Him reveal to you His wisdom and His understanding.

You are probably familiar with 2 Corinthians 5:17: *Therefore if any man be **in Christ**, he is a new creature: old things are passed away; behold, all things are become new.* Are you **in Christ?** If so, then you are committed to Colossians 2:2,3: *That their hearts might be comforted, being knit together in love, and unto all riches of the full assurance of understanding, to the acknowledgment of the mystery of God, and of the Father, and of Christ; **In whom are hid all the treasures of wisdom and knowledge.*** We read earlier from Proverbs that one hand of Wisdom holds riches and honor and the other hand holds length of days. These are **some** of the treasures of Wisdom — **all** of them are hid **in Christ**. Wisdom is in Christ. You are in Christ. Wisdom is in you! It belongs to you! Welcome to where the riches are!

In financial dealings, the truly wise man, one who is operating in the covenant of God, will not borrow money. He will not obligate himself in this way. A man who borrows money is relying on the world's system of finance and will never be in absolute control of his affairs. God has a system of finance which will provide everything you need. It is not a sin to borrow money, but there is a better way. Why not use it? There is a higher life. Reach for it!

This is a very difficult area where businessmen are concerned, but God can and will provide everything any businessman can conceive in his heart or mind. God has a way! This is something you grow into spiritually. If you want to believe God for thousands of dollars to operate your business, you will have to start by believing Him for your next shirt and tie. As you do, you will grow into a position where you can believe Him to provide large amounts of money. The wisdom of God will cause these things to happen, and it comes forth only by spending time in the Word.

Suppose Henry Ford walked up, handed you a book, and said, "This book contains every secret that I have learned in the automobile industry, in the manufacturing business, and in the stock market. It has been tried and proven over a period of years to produce absolutely if you will read it one hour each day and meditate in it." Would you trade an hour's sleep for the success Henry Ford enjoyed? This and so much more is available to you by reading and meditating in the Word of God. Commit yourself to it. Make up your mind and heart before God.

It is the responsibility of every member of the Body of Christ to believe God for the abundance He provides. When one of us falls short in this responsibility, the whole Body of Christ suffers because of that one cell. (You may not use your little finger very much, but if it is sore, your whole hand suffers.) As believers, we have a responsibility to provide for the needs of our brothers and sisters around the world. If we lack, they will suffer for it.

Now you can see that the basic reason for the operation of faith is **to meet the needs of mankind.** You may not need much money to be happy and successful in your own life, but people are starving and dying throughout the world. Someone must provide for them. They don't know how to get it for themselves. There are even preachers going hungry! The biggest complaint from people is that all the preachers are wanting money. Do you know the best way to stop that complaint? Give to them! Don't get into strife with them; bless them with your giving and pray for them.

The covenant is yours. The wisdom of God is yours. It resides within you. Bring it to the surface by meditating in the Word of God and giving God the opportunity to share His system with you. When you let Him be your Source of supply, you can live independently from the world's system. The Word states so plainly in 2 Corinthians that without aid or support you can continue to be generous in every good work. This is the attitude God is looking for. This man is **unlimited** in the things of the Lord. Praise God!

When we began plans for our first television series, people said that we couldn't do it because of the tremendous cost of such an operation. One man offered us, at half price, an estimate of $750 per finished minute. For a sixty-minute program, the total production cost would have been $45,000. The thought of financing a weekly series for one year at that price was overwhelming! For a series of five programs, they quoted us $350,000. Then the Lord said, "Why don't you give **Me** a chance? You've asked the experts about it; now let Me in on it!" So I did. God moved—and we filmed the five-part series for $3,750! The apostle Paul said, ...*the world is crucified unto me, and I unto the world* (Gal. 6:14).

The first and most important rule for you to follow in operating in the power of God and living by faith is this: One hundred percent committal to the Word of God and its authority in your life. As God told Joshua, the best way to prosper is by meditation in the Word. Don't just study it; there is a difference between meditation and study. Study involves digging in the Word, running references in a concordance, and so forth; but meditation many times covers only two or three verses of scripture. Read a verse several times. Roll it over in your mind; be quiet and listen to God for twenty or thirty minutes. This has been the way I have learned many things about the Word and about Jesus' ministry. The Spirit of God can say enough in one sentence to last you a month! He was sent here to teach us the deep things of God (see 1 Cor. 2:9,10).

Let me give you an example from my own experience. Some time ago, I decided to find out how to operate financially according to the Word of God. I believed that God had a financial system that most Christians did not know. This was evident in my dad's life. My parents decided when they married that they would tithe their income for the rest of their lives. They knew very little about believing God for finances. My dad relied on his ability to work. He was an excellent sales representative and God blessed his business. When I entered the ministry and started studying the Word of God, I read where God said to bring the tithes into the storehouse and He would **open the windows of heaven** (see Mal. 3:10). Well, I could look at my dad and see that this wasn't working in his life. He made more than a good living, but he worked for every dime he got! So I began to study this and question the Lord about it.

One thing that He showed me was the pride element in most businessmen, especially the ones who worked hard like Dad. You couldn't give my dad anything; **he** was the giver! If God wanted to give him something, He had to channel it through the business or Dad would actually get uncomfortable and embarrassed if someone tried to give to him. This is wrong. God showed me that most businessmen don't know how to receive simply because of their pride.

I had been praying in the Spirit, praying in tongues, for several hours one day in preparation for a meeting and the Lord spoke to my heart. He said, "I want you to teach these people on tithing." I said, "What do you mean? I don't know anything about it myself!" All I knew was that the word **tithe** meant ten percent! I tithed because that's what I had been taught at home and in church. (Two things I knew—get saved and tithe. We heard sermons for 50 weeks each year on salvation and the other two on tithing!) Well, I continued to pray and the Lord kept bringing up the subject of tithing. Finally I said, "If You want me to teach on tithing, You'll have to teach me first." He said, "Turn in My Word to where I introduced it, and I'll show you." So I began to meditate in these scriptures. I would read from the Word, then close my eyes, and listen to God. If my mind started to wander, I would go back to the Word and read it again and again and again and think about it and listen to God some more. You need to spend time listening to God! What will you pay for success?

In fellowshipping with God around the Word, I began to learn some things. God has His system under wraps, hidden in the Word, and meditation is the key to the mystery. This way Satan can't get his hands on it. (Later in the book I will share some of these secrets on tithing with you.)

One time I was meditating about Peter catching the fish with the money in its mouth. I realized this was a financial operation, so I decided to find out what God had to say. I must have read that story 50 times and ran into a blank wall each time! I could see that Peter needed tax money and Jesus told him to go fishing. He caught the fish and got the money out of its mouth. I would run that through my thinking, sometimes for hours, then get up and say, "Well, Lord, I know it's here somewhere, and by faith, I claim the revelation on it!" Finally, in prayer one day I picked up my Bible, flipped it open to that passage, and read it once more. Then I saw something I had read over and over again. Jesus said, "Get the money out of the mouth of the **first** fish." Peter was going to catch a mess of fish! Then the Lord spoke to my heart and said, "Son, don't bind Me to finances. I can handle the fish just as I can the money." I saw what I had been missing! I had been centering on the one fish. Now if I had been in Peter's place, I would have jerked the money out of the fish's mouth, run down to pay the taxes, and then realized that I didn't have anything to eat. I would have been so short-sighted that I would have thrown the fish back and missed out on the rest of the catch. If there was a first fish, there had to be a second and so on. Peter was a commercial fisherman and knew how to market those fish. Jesus obviously loaded his boat again. I would have spent part of the money on something to eat and still couldn't have paid my taxes. I thought, "I have been believing for the money to buy an automobile when I should have been believing God for the automobile itself!" The Lord said, "That's right. You have had Me bound to that little channel of money." Then He said something I'll never forget, "Son, if I send you a cow with a bag of money around her neck, for goodness' sake, milk her before you send her home!" The Lord has a tremendous sense of humor, but I didn't know it until I began to fellowship with Him and meditate in His Word.

### The Rich Young Ruler

There is another area that I want to share with you about God's financial system. In Mark 10:17-23, we find the story of the rich young ruler. This is one of the most misunderstood incidents in the whole Bible. We have read this in the light of the world's traditional system, thinking God wanted to break that young man but this is not so. We have misunderstood it for the same reason that the rich young ruler missed God—ignorance of the Word of God. He did not know what the covenant said. He knew "the Law" and the Ten Commandments, but the Abrahamic Covenant covered much more than these. God made an agreement with Abraham and promised to do certain things if he would obey the Word; then the prophets were raised up to add to this covenant and record it for Israel to use. Let's read Mark's account of this conversation.

*And when he was gone forth into the way, there came one running, and kneeled to him, and asked him, Good Master, what shall I do that I may inherit eternal life? And Jesus said unto him, Why callest thou me good? there is none good but one, that is, God. Thou knowest the commandments, Do not commit adultery, Do not kill, Do not steal, Do not bear false witness, Defraud not, Honour thy father and mother. And he answered and said unto him, Master, all these have I observed from my youth. Then Jesus beholding him loved him, and said unto him, One thing thou lackest: go thy way, sell whatsoever thou hast, and give to the poor, and thou shalt have treasure in heaven: and come, take up the cross, and follow me. And he was sad at that saying, and went away grieved: for he had great possessions. And Jesus looked round about, and saith unto his disciples, How hardly shall they that have riches enter into the kingdom of God!*

Before you begin meditation in the Word, you must commit yourself to the absolute truth of John 10:10. *The thief cometh not, but for to steal, and to kill, and to destroy: I am come that they might have life, and that they might have it more abundantly.* Whenever I read something that seems contradictory to this, I immediately stop and straighten out my thinking. The truth is hidden in some way, and I rely on the Holy Spirit to reveal it to me. God is not our problem. He does not steal from us. He is the Giver of all good things! When you commit yourself to this basic truth, you block Satan and deal a deadly blow to deception. As long as you are open to it, Satan will prove that God wants you to live in poverty and in sickness to teach you humility. He will try to convince you that the rich young ruler couldn't receive eternal life because he had money, but Satan is a liar and the father of lies!

Here is how the Lord revealed the truth to me: As I read Mark 10:20, *And he answered and said unto him, Master, all these have I observed FROM MY YOUTH,* the Lord spoke to me and said, "See, this is why he was rich." Then He pointed me to Deuteronomy 8:18 about the Lord giving power to get wealth in order to establish His covenant. This young man was evidently walking in this part of the covenant. The Lord said, "Do you think I would ask something from him that I hadn't given him in the first place?" You must realize these two facts: (1) God is the only reason you have anything, and (2) He will never ask you to give up something without giving you something better in return.

Verse 21 says, *Then Jesus beholding him loved him.* Now some people think that God doesn't like people with money, but this says that when Jesus looked at that young man, He loved him...**before** He said anything about giving away his possessions. You see, He loved him and what He said was to the man's advantage.

Then the story continues with, *Jesus...said unto him, One thing thou lackest.* What he lacked was a working revelation of the covenant. The young man only did as he was supposed to. He presented himself as knowing the Word, and Jesus tested his knowledge by saying, *Go thy way, sell whatsoever thou hast, and give to the poor, and thou shalt have treasure in heaven: and come, take up the cross, and follow me.* What did the young man do? He walked off sadly because he had great possessions. Jesus could have stopped him right then and explained what He meant, but if He had, the man would have obeyed in the natural and not by faith. If he had asked Jesus to explain Himself, He would have. Each time His disciples asked Him to explain a parable, He did, but He never explained it in order to get them to act on it. If the man had really known the covenant, he would have thought, "What does the covenant say about giving to the poor?" He would have remembered Proverbs 19:17 that says, *He that hath pity upon the poor lendeth unto the Lord; and that which he hath given will he pay him again.* This was the biggest financial deal that young man had ever been offered, but he walked away from it because he didn't know God's system of finance. He didn't take the time to inquire; he just **assumed** that God wanted to break him. Instead of being Word-minded that young man was money-minded.

When the rich young ruler walked away, Jesus said, *How hardly shall they that have riches enter into the kingdom of God!* Then an interesting thing happened. The next verse says, *And the disciples were **astonished** at his words.* We have just taken it for granted that Jesus and His disciples didn't have anything. But the Bible describes Peter, James, and John as professional fishermen. They owned more than one boat, and they had household servants! When Jesus spoke those words, it shook them. It was adverse to what they had seen. **They were astonished at His words!** Jesus was not poor in His ministry. He had a treasurer! Turn off your religious head and read the Word of God as if it were your newspaper.

Another point I want you to grasp is the reality of Jesus' words, *Come, take up the cross, and follow me.* What does "the cross" refer to? "The cross we are to bear" is selfish, unlovely people. The greatest commandment is that we love one another. Unfortunately, some people are not easy to love, but we are to love them anyway. We are to bear one another's burdens and uphold one another. We must stop strife with the love of God. This is our cross. Do you realize the significance of His words, *Come...follow me?* These are the words Jesus spoke to every man He commissioned as an apostle. When I saw this, the Lord said,

"Wouldn't this man have been the logical replacement for Judas?" Judas failed because of the love of money. He even stole from the bag! This young ruler was an excellent businessman; he was honest and had operated the covenant from his youth. He was perfect for the job, but he turned his back on this tremendous opportunity to follow Jesus.

Now let's read on from Mark 10:25. *It is easier for a camel to go through the eye of a needle, than for a rich man to enter into the kingdom of God. And they were astonished out of measure, saying among themselves, Who then can be saved? And Jesus looking upon them saith, With men it is impossible, but not with God: for with God all things are possible. Then Peter began to say unto him, Lo, we have left all, and have followed thee. And Jesus answered and said, Verily I say unto you, There is no man that hath left house, or brethren, or sisters, or father, or mother, or wife, or children, or lands, for my sake, and the gospel's, But he shall receive an hundredfold **now in this time.*** IN THIS LIFE! He intended to give the rich young ruler a hundred times what he had!

Jesus said, *...an hundredfold now in this time, houses, and brethren, and sisters, and mothers, and children, and lands, with persecutions; and in the world to come eternal life.* The moment God begins to bless you, you will get persecuted because you become dangerous to Satan. You begin to know that God is the Source of your success, that He is the one giving it to you, that there is an endless supply behind you and an endless supply in front of you. All you must do is be a channel for it **and giving is the key that opens the door.** Jesus knew the spiritual law of giving, and He operated it proficiently. He gave to the poor at such an astonishing rate that when Judas left the room during the Last Supper, some people thought that he must be going to give to the poor.

Do you want a hundredfold return on your money? Give and let God multiply it back to you. No bank in the world offers this kind of return! Praise the Lord!

This is operating and using what the Bible calls "the royal law." **Love your neighbor as yourself.** Be as quick to care for the needs of others as you are your own needs. The world knows it exists; they call it "the Golden Rule," but they don't understand how it functions and neither do most Christians.

This whole system of finance must be operated by faith in order for it to function properly. My dad was tithing as God had said, but he was not believing for the return on his giving. He had it stacked up in heaven, yet he was getting no benefit from it here on earth. Finally, when he learned some of these things, he started believing God and he is better off financially today in retirement than he was when he worked so hard. He began to mix his faith with God's Word concerning finances. There are many tithers who say, "Why, I couldn't ask God to give anything back to me!" This shows that they don't really know what the Word says about tithing. When God introduced tithing in the Book of Deuteronomy, He commanded the people to say to Him, "Look down from thy holy habitation and bless your people with a land that flows with milk and honey." They were commanded to say this to the Lord!

Remember, the basic fundamental law for establishing your heart in the covenant of God is meditation in the Word. You must commit yourself to the fact that God's Word works. **Meditation is fixing your mind on the Word.** Here are seven steps to help you learn how to meditate God's Word:

1. Apply the Word to you personally.
2. Allow the Holy Spirit to make God's Word a reality in your heart.
3. Carefully ponder how this Word applies to your life.
4. Dwell on how this Word from the Lord changes your situation.

5. Place yourself in agreement with what God's Word says about you.
6. See yourself as God sees you.
7. Begin to realize the integrity of God's Word.

You must commit yourself to the fact that God's Word is true and that it works!

## Chapter Three
# *Your Heavenly Account*

*Lay not up for yourselves treasures upon earth, where moth and rust doth corrupt, and where thieves break through and steal: but lay up for yourselves treasures in heaven, where neither moth nor rust doth corrupt, and where thieves do not break through nor steal: For where your treasure is, there will your heart be also. The light of the body is the eye: if therefore thine eye be single, thy whole body shall be full of light. But if thine eye be evil, thy whole body shall be full of darkness. If therefore the light that is in thee be darkness, how great is that darkness!* (Matt. 6:19-23).

You need to have a single eye, to become single-minded, concerning the Word of God. You must accept God's Word as final authority. What it says, it means. When the Word says you are healed, **you are healed!** It doesn't matter what your body says about it. If you will believe this and operate accordingly, then the covenant you have with God — His Word — will become the absolute truth in your situation, and your physical body will come into agreement with the Word.

I first began to learn this in the area of finance and prosperity when I went back to college. The idea of going back to school really scared me! I was thirty years old with a wife, two small children, and no idea how I would support them. There were people who told me I was making a mistake, that my family would go hungry, but I had accepted the call to the ministry and was looking to the **Lord** to meet my needs. Many people thought I was nuts! According to the world's system, a man has to be in sheer poverty while he is in college, but the Word doesn't say that. It doesn't say, "God will meet your needs according to His riches in glory just as soon as you get out of college." At that time I knew very little about operating by faith, but I was doggedly determined to go through with it. God took care of us. I never asked anybody for a quarter. We began to learn how to operate by faith.

In Matthew 6:20, Jesus teaches us to *lay up for yourselves treasures in heaven, where neither moth nor rust doth corrupt, and where thieves do not break through nor steal.* This is what the Word says. However, with our **religious** heads we have read it this way: "Lay not up for yourselves treasures on earth...but lay up for yourselves treasures in heaven, where neither moth nor rust doth corrupt...**and where thou canst not touch it until thou gettest to heaven.**" We have added our own little idea, but this is not what Jesus meant. He was saying, "If you will let heaven be your treasury and your supply, then regardless of what happens on earth, you will have a bank that is not subject to theft or ruin." What you have laid up then will be ready when it is needed. Jesus was not referring to when we get to heaven. He was teaching about God providing for us **now.** If you will notice, He finished His sermon in the sixth chapter of Matthew by saying that your heavenly Father knows you need these things, but seek first the kingdom of God and His righteousness and all these other things will be added to you.

First Timothy 6:17-19 illustrates this same point. *Charge them that are rich in this world, that they be not highminded, nor trust in uncertain riches, but in the living God, who giveth us richly all things to enjoy; That they do good, that they be rich in good works, ready to distribute, willing to communicate; Laying up in store for themselves a good foundation against the time to come, that they may lay hold on eternal life.*

*Charge them that are rich in this world, that they be not highminded, nor trust in uncertain riches.* Paul was referring to those who are rich here on earth—that they should not trust in their riches. This is the reason Jesus said it was hard for a rich man to enter the kingdom of God. When a rich man trusts in his money, his heart will be in his riches. Satan then will be able to deceive him; the deceitfulness of riches will choke the Word of God and cause it to become unfruitful in him (see Mark 4:19).

*Nor trust in uncertain riches, but in the living God, who giveth us richly all things to enjoy; That they do good, that they be rich in good works, ready to distribute, willing to communicate; Laying up in store for themselves a good foundation against the time to come, that they may lay hold on eternal life.* You don't lay hold on eternal life after you get to heaven. You lay hold on it **by faith** while you are here on earth, taking a firm stand and standing fast in the liberty into which you are called. The Twenty-third Psalm speaks of God preparing a feast before us, and we have thought of this as a heavenly feast. However, it says He is preparing a table before us **in the presence of our enemies.** Our enemies are not in heaven. They are here on earth! When the Lord showed me this, He said, "The only problem I have is getting My kids to come to the table!" Paul tells us to "lay up in store" for ourselves in our heavenly bank account by being "ready to distribute" and "willing to communicate." Then when we need it, we have it on deposit in heaven! ALL the money, gold, etc., is already in the earth. By giving, heaven declares certain portions as mine. No force on earth then is able to keep it from coming to me when I call for it! Heaven's record says so, and earth dares not refuse.

While I was in prayer one afternoon during a meeting in Dayton, Ohio, the Lord drew me to this portion of scripture about laying up treasures in heaven where neither moth nor rust corrupts. As I read this, the Lord said, "This rust and corruption is inflation and depression." If you will let heaven be your financial reservoir—your bank and depository where you place your trust—regardless of what happens to the world's system, you will always have more than enough! Then the Lord said, "I did not say this treasure could not be used until you get to heaven." First Timothy 6:19 says to lay up for yourselves a good foundation **for the time to come when you will need it.** A heavenly bank is not subject to theft and ruin; it will always be there when you need it.

Up to this time I was under the impression that when I gave, I could expect the entire amount plus the hundred-fold return on it immediately, but there were times when it didn't work like that. I was confused, so I asked the Lord about it. **My needs were always abundantly met,** but I didn't fully understand what was happening. The Lord explained it this way:

"There was no use in My transferring money which you had laid up in heaven to an earthly bank when you didn't need all of it at the time. When money is on earth, it is vulnerable to Satan and to the world's system of finance. If I gave you one thousand dollars today, in nine months time, it probably wouldn't be worth more than seven hundred fifty dollars. You need to learn to exercise your faith in the fact that you have this money on deposit, and when you need it, all you have to do is call for it. Make your deposits with Me according to the rate of exchange which My Word guarantees and operate under My system of finance instead of the world's system. We can make it work at the current rate of exchange at that time. It won't matter if it takes a billion dollars to buy a loaf of bread—I [God] can afford it!" If God can afford it, so can I. He's my Father!

While I was in Ohio, God dealt with me about the television ministry. At that time I could not understand, or see, with my own mind how it would work financially, but I had learned long before not to back off for this reason. I knew the Lord could work it out. It didn't matter how it operated or what the financial details were, I knew there was only one way to succeed—by giving. Then the thought flashed across my mind, "No man has given until he has given all he has," and the first thing I saw was my twin-engine airplane. Well, cold chills ran up and down my spine! That little plane was my pride and joy. I had tithed and believed God for it, and He had given it to me as a tool of this ministry. Because of this, it really meant a lot to me. Then I realized that I had to get rid of it. I couldn't afford to let it come between God and me, so I went into prayer and the Lord said, "If you will realize what I am leading you into, you will make an agreement with Me so that I can help you financially. Make Me Lord over your finances." That is exactly what I did. I wrote out an agreement about the airplane and used it to lay up a treasure in heaven for the time to come when I would need it. I didn't want to release that airplane, but I knew that God would not take it without His giving more in return. My faith dictated that God's Word was true, so I disciplined my thinking to get in line with my faith (instead of my fear) and I wrote out this agreement: "On the fourth day of October 1971, I give my airplane to the Lord to be sold and the money put into preaching the Word of God on television and in any other manner possible."

I made this covenant with the Lord according to Luke 6:38, *Give, and it shall be given unto you...again,* and Mark 10:30, *But he shall receive an hundredfold now in this time.* The agreement also contained this statement: "I freely give this money from the sale of the airplane, and I expect the return on it."

Then I had the engines overhauled, had some maintenance done, ran an annual inspection on it, and altogether spent about eight thousand dollars on a piece of equipment that technically didn't belong to me any longer. Since God is love, it follows that the laws governing the power of God are the giving laws. You can't stop these laws and still make God's power operate. It just will not work that way! God's system is really unique. He takes a person who is absolutely destitute, provides the seed to start his giving, then gives him the hundredfold return on what he gives. Only God could manage or afford a financial operation like that!

I made the agreement to release my airplane in October 1971. Then on February 11, 1972, while we were holding a meeting in Birmingham, Alabama, the Lord instructed me to give it to a particular evangelist. So that is what I did. This is the point I want you to grasp: When God told me to give it away, I didn't hesitate for one moment. You see, God had set up this deal almost four months before, and there had been time for me to be healed of a possessive spirit where that plane was concerned. Therefore, when God spoke, I acted and was thrilled to do it! We flew it home and gave it away.

My schedule was already set up, and it dictated that I use an airplane. You can't operate on our schedule and use the airlines or an automobile. It was set up around a private plane. Airlines service 650 airports in the United States. We service eight thousand with our own plane. So you can see that there was an immediate need for another airplane.

God said, "When you give the airplane, this deposit will enable you to call for a withdrawal to handle your television ministry." Well, in order to film it and put it on the air before the people, we needed several months time and thousands of dollars. The Lord had already shown me how it was to operate—the people who heard the Word would support it in order for others to hear it. But there was a certain period of time when the television ministry would not be exposed to anyone. This created a need in addition to the need for an airplane. The Lord said, "I'll handle it for you if you'll make the proper deposits." So we did.

On the twenty-first day of February, just ten days later, we had a new airplane and the money for the television ministry. Just ten days! Only *God* could handle a situation like that. The second airplane was worth five times more than the first one. It was larger and faster, flew higher and farther. In fact, it was exactly the plane that I had asked for, and all the bills were paid! Praise the Lord!

Your Heavenly Account

We need to learn how to make the proper deposits in our heavenly bank so that we can withdraw from it when needed. Once you realize you have this on deposit, it will become easy to believe God for it. Your faith will work easier. It's not difficult to believe God for the money you have on deposit at the corner bank. You don't have to exercise your faith to write a check on it. But it takes a considerable amount of faith to get money when you don't have any on deposit. The same principle works with God. The reason this action took place so fast in my case was because the deposit had already been made. It was there in heaven and available on call. There are many people who have made these deposits with God and have never called for them because they don't realize they are laid up in store for them *now*.

## Depositing in Your Heavenly Account

There are four major areas we can use in giving, or making deposits in heaven: tithing, giving to the poor, investing in the gospel, and giving as a praise to God. We will discuss each of these and learn the principles on which they operate. It is very important for you to realize that these are distinctly different although they overlap in some ways. Each has an individual set of laws governing it from the Word with its own return. For instance, tithing is not the same as investing in the gospel. Tithing is an investment in God. It is the part of your income that belongs to Him and goes directly to Him. As a tither, you have certain privileges which we will discuss now.

## Tithing

This is, of course, the most familiar financial subject to Christians. Nearly all of us are aware of the practice of tithing, but very few actually realize its true significance. It was a commandment of God to Israel and ten percent of their firstfruits belonged to God. As I mentioned earlier, when God told me to teach this subject for the first time, He led me to chapter 26 of Deuteronomy where He first introduced it to Israel. Let's start with the first verse and relate this to our role under the New Covenant.

*And it shall be, when thou art come in unto the land which the Lord thy God giveth thee for an inheritance, and possessest it, and dwellest therein.* How does this relate to the Christian? The Word says in Colossians 1:13 that God has delivered us from the power of darkness and has translated us into the kingdom of His dear Son. We are living in the kingdom of God. We have entered into our inheritance in Jesus Christ and possess it in His name. We have the title deed to this kingdom through faith in Jesus Christ. The authority has been given to us, and God is showing us how to exercise our tithing privileges in order to maintain control efficiently in the financial world.

Verses 2,3, *That thou shalt take of the first of all the fruit of the earth, which thou shalt bring of thy land that the Lord thy God giveth thee, and shalt put it in a basket, and shalt go unto the place which the Lord thy God shall choose to place his name there. And thou shalt go unto the priest that shall be in those days.* Who is this priest? Hebrews 3:1 says that Jesus is our High Priest. Hebrews 7:8, speaking of Jesus, says He receives our tithes personally. Therefore, we are to go to Him with our tithes and say to Him, "I profess this day unto the Lord God that I am come into the inheritance which the Lord swore to give me." This is a very important point in the tithing procedure: **Make a confession before your High Priest.**

Verse 4, *And the priest shall take the basket out of thine hand, and set it down before the altar of the Lord thy God.* Can you see where we have been missing it? We quickly drop our tithe money into the offering plate as it passes by or stuff it into an envelope without a thought. Instead, we are to present it to Jesus, who, in turn, will set it before the altar of God.

Then in verses 5-10, the Lord builds Israel a confession telling of His mighty work in their lives and of delivering them from bondage in Egypt. At this point, we Christians need to switch to our position under the New Testament. We were sinners in the world, and our confession should be something like this: "I am in the land which You have provided for me in Jesus Christ, the kingdom of Almighty God. I was a sinner serving Satan. He was my god. But I called upon the name of Jesus, and You heard my cry and delivered me from the power and authority of darkness and translated me into the kingdom of Your dear Son. Jesus is my Lord, and I bring the firstfruits of my labors to Him as the High Priest and worship You with it. We rejoice in all the good which You have given to us and our household."

This is *our* confession of redemption equivalent to Israel's deliverance from Egypt. The Bible says this is a type of our deliverance from Satan. Israel pointed to Egypt; we point to Calvary. Now as a guide for you to use, we have set out this entire confession based on Deuteronomy 26:

We profess this day unto the Lord God that we have come into the inheritance which the Lord swore to give us. We are in the land which You have provided for us in Jesus Christ, the kingdom of Almighty God. We were sinners serving Satan. He was our god. But we called upon the name of Jesus, and You heard our cry and delivered us from the power and authority of darkness and translated us into the kingdom of Your dear Son.

Jesus, as our Lord and High Priest, we bring the firstfruits of our income to You and worship the Lord our God with it. We rejoice in all the good which You have given to us and our household. We have hearkened to the voice of the Lord our God and have done according to all that He has commanded us.

Now look down from Your holy habitation, from heaven, and bless us as You said in Your Word.

All of this is involved in tithing. You can readily see that it can't be done in the few seconds before the plate is passed in church. It must be done on purpose, but I guarantee you, it is worth every minute of it! My wife and I write our tithe checks, hold them before God, and take the time to pray over them. Our money then becomes a tool used in worshipping God.

Deuteronomy 26:10 says that the high priest will set the tithes before God and worship Him with them. Can you grasp Jesus worshipping God with your money? Wow! That's quite a picture.

There is another part of this confession, from verses 14,15, which is very important: *I have hearkened to the voice of the Lord my God, and have done according to all that thou hast commanded me. Look down from thy holy habitation, from heaven, and bless thy people Israel, and the land which thou hast given us, as thou swarest unto our fathers, a land that floweth with milk and honey.* In contrast, we have thought, "I'll just keep giving and maybe one of these days He will notice it and bless me." This is wrong. The blessing of God is received by faith in His Word. It does not come automatically, just as salvation does not come automatically. You could say, "Well, go to church and God will save you one of these days, if you're lucky!" No, the laws governing salvation must be acted on in order for them to work in your life. *Prosperity comes the same way.* As we can see in Malachi 3:10,11, God has promised the tither that He will open the windows of heaven and pour out a blessing that there will not be room enough to receive.

We had an opportunity to put this to work some years ago when a friend of mine had come to a standstill in his construction business. He hadn't received a contract in a long time and something had to be done, so he and his wife came to us for prayer. As I was praying about his situation, the Lord showed me how to handle the problem. He was a tither, so we used what was his according to the Word in Malachi 3:10,11, *Bring ye all the tithes into the store-house, that there may be meat in mine house, and prove me now herewith, saith the Lord of hosts, if I will not open you the windows of heaven, and pour you out a blessing, that there shall not be room enough to receive it. And I will rebuke the devourer for your sakes, and he shall not destroy the fruits of your ground; neither shall your vine cast her fruit before the time in the field.* We prayed in line with this and believed God for an abundant blessing. Then we rebuked the devourer, Satan. We said, "Satan, this man is a tither, and you have no right to bind his business. In the name of Jesus, we command you to get your hands off and do it now!" When I spoke with him about three months later, he said that business had begun to pour in. Praise the Lord! These are our rights as tithers according to the Word of God.

In tithing, you are laying the foundation for financial success and abundance. You are establishing deposits with God that can be used when you need them. Don't wait until your back is against the wall before you use your faith in this area. Build your faith first when things are going well. Learn to act on the Word now, and when Satan tries to pin you against the wall, you can smile and know that you have it made. His power over you financially has been stopped! When you stand on the covenant of God and exercise your rights as a tither, Satan has no chance against you. God will rebuke the devourer for your sake. If your back is against the wall financially now, *don't wait to begin tithing.* You cannot afford to wait! The tithe belongs to God in the first place. *Will a man rob God? Yet ye have robbed me. But ye say, Wherein have we robbed thee? In tithes and offerings. Ye are cursed with a curse: for ye have robbed me* (Mal. 3:8,9). This scripture says that a man who does not tithe is robbing God and is operating under a curse because of it. Start tithing now! If you don't have any money, find something you do have and give it today. There is no faster or surer way to break that curse. Immediately when money comes into your hands, FIRST take God's tithe out and present it to Him. *Honor the Lord with your capital and sufficiency [from righteous labors], and with the first fruits of all your income, So shall your storage places be filled with plenty, and your vats be overflowing with new wine* (Prov. 3:9,10, *Amplified*).

Remember, the Word says that God gives us the power to get wealth and the blessing of the Lord makes rich. In tithing, God is giving you 90 percent and receiving for His work in the earth 10 percent to **provide ministry for you.** *And he gave some, apostles; and some, prophets; and some, evangelists; and some, pastors and teachers; For the perfecting of the saints, for the work of the ministry, for the edifying of the body of Christ* (Eph. 4:11,12). You can't out give God! He gives back His ten percent to see to it that you are perfected, equipped, and edified.

This brings us to the question of where God's tithes are to be placed. Some think only churches are to receive tithes. This would be true if their church is the source of their spiritual food and growth. The Word says to bring the tithes into the storehouse so that there would be MEAT in His house. A storehouse is where the food is. I know thousands of people attending churches of all denominations that receive no spiritual food whatsoever from their churches. How could that be a storehouse?

Verse 14 of Deuteronomy 26 *Amplified* says, *I have not eaten of the tithe…or given any of it to the dead; I have hearkened to the voice of the Lord my God, and have done according to all that You have commanded me.* I would not consider putting God's tithe into a dead work. If you want to put money in a church that is dead—not ministering to people—then put *your* money into it, but it is important to put the tithe into a storehouse that is feeding the life of God to the people. Many churches and foundations serve as Satan's reservoir to keep finances out of the revival that is in the earth today.

To settle this question, since it is God's money to start with and since Jesus is the One who will handle and receive the tithe (see Heb. 7:8), pray and let Him tell you where it should be put to work. I realize this is not too popular with some church doctrines, but nevertheless, it is accurate. Jesus is Lord over the finances of the Body of Christ! He is fair, and He is just in the distribution of God's tithe. When a church sees to it that the people are fed, that church will receive its portion. When an evangelist sees to it that the people are fed, Jesus will minister to him his portion of God's tithe. All the different ministries qualify to receive from Jesus more than enough to fulfill their particular calling **when they feed God's people.**

### Giving to the Poor

The second form of depositing is giving to the poor. Proverbs 19:17 says, *He that hath pity upon the poor lendeth unto the Lord; and that which he hath given will he pay him again.* When you give to the poor, you can expect back what you gave. You can't give away your money by giving to the poor. You are actually lending to the Lord, and He will repay you. He considers it a loan, and since He teaches us not to owe money, He won't owe money either. As soon as you lend it to Him, He will pay it back. If Jesus walked up to you and asked to borrow one hundred dollars, don't you think He would repay you!

It is important for you to realize that all material wealth is in the earth. It will not be rained down on us from heaven. **It is already here, and there is more than enough for everyone.** The Bible says that we will suck of the abundance of the seas and of the treasures hid in the sand (see Deut. 33:19). The problem is that we don't know how to reach it. However, by giving to the poor we are giving God an opportunity not only to work with us financially and bless us, but also to help the man in need.

There are some things you need to understand about this form of giving. I remember when a close friend of mine was telling me about taking some things to a poor woman. She said, "You know, before I could even get out the door, the woman was asking if I had any pots and pans or anything else she could have." This attitude of the poor woman disturbed her, so we prayed about it. The Lord spoke to me and said, "That's the way you do Me. I give you one thing, and before long you're jerking My coattail over something else. Now that's all right with Me, but you must realize that you are the only hope a poor person has. You represent supply to them and they have never had that before."

This puts a different light on the subject. The poor consider this a rich man's world. Satan has dominated them with poverty and suppression of all kinds. When you realize that Satan is behind their oppression, you will see their need for the power of God in their lives. Then you won't be afraid to obligate them to the gospel when you give material things to them. Whenever I give in this way, I always explain what the Word says and tell them about Jesus. I let them know that Jesus is my source of supply and is willing to be theirs. Show them that they, too, can become God's channel in the earth to someone else. You see, you can feed a thief all day long, but all you will have is a thief full of food. The food won't change him, but the Word of God will transform him on the inside. If you give to the poor in the proper way, then you can witness to them and introduce them to the power of God. I never give to the poor without telling them about Jesus. If they are to get my material goods, they will first have to listen to what I have to say about Jesus.

Jesus taught about giving alms, which is giving to the poor. Evidently, Jesus was well-known for giving to the poor from the scriptural accounts of His ministry. In the Sermon on the Mount, Jesus taught about giving alms. He said, *Let not thy left hand know what thy right hand doeth*

(Matt. 6:3). You can get more fun out of giving to someone anonymously! It is a joy you will never get from anything else, and the next verse says, *And thy Father which seeth in secret himself shall reward thee openly.* HE HIMSELF shall reward you. Praise the Lord for His generous propositions!

## Investing in the Gospel

As we have read in Mark 10:29,30, Jesus said, *Verily I say unto you, There is no man that hath left house, or brethren, or sisters, or father, or mother, or wife, or children, or lands, for my sake, and the gospel's, But he shall receive an hundredfold now in this time.* This is an investment in spreading the gospel throughout the world. The Great Commission says, *Go ye into all the world, and preach the gospel to every creature* (Mark 16:15). We all are obligated to this; and if we can't go, we are to send someone in our place. Everyone is to function in this Commission. The missionary is an apostle of God, an instrument to evangelize the world. Unfortunately, he has been grossly underrated and occupies the bottom rung of the ladder instead of the top. However, they deserve our support both in finances and in prayer. God will support the communication of the gospel with whatever power and resources it takes. Unless the Word is preached, there is no faith (see Rom. 10:14). Without faith, no one is saved (see Eph. 2:8). To the man who has never heard the Word, Jesus has never died. You can see that if God did not support communication of the gospel, the cross would have been in vain.

Another area to invest in the gospel is supporting ministries that are assigned the job of teaching God's people how to function in spiritual affairs. The teaching ministries have a great responsibility placed on them by God. Consequently, they are greatly blessed.

Any investment expert will be quick to tell you that the most productive form of investing is a steady, regular investment into solid business. There is nothing more solid than God's work! Begin to be a regular investor. Be faithful to it.

Let's go back to what Jesus said in Mark 10:29,30. He has said that this will work for **every** man. Peter had said, "What about us? We have left all and have followed you." He asked this as if he thought Jesus' staff stood in some special place where these laws are concerned. Jesus answered him in no uncertain terms. Every man who invests into the gospel has a right to expect the staggering return of one hundredfold.

## Giving as a Praise to God

Just as Israel made sacrificial offerings of praise to God, believers today can use giving as an instrument of praise. It is interesting to note that Israel never gave a blemished animal as a sacrifice. In light of this, if you give a second-hand pair of shoes, then that is what you will get in return. Don't give your old worn-out things; give your good things and you'll never lack good things. This is what I did by giving my airplane; it was the best thing I had at the time.

A few years ago an evangelist came to me and said, "I don't understand it, but my income has completely stopped. I haven't had a dime come in for weeks!" Since I had just preached that morning on Luke 6:38, I told him that the key was giving and that he should give whatever he had; if not money, then something else. He went home and gathered up all his clothes (except one suit, one sport coat, and one pair of slacks), passed them out to the men at the unemployment office, and preached the Word to them. When he came to the meeting that night, he was beaming. He had given as a praise to God and was really high because of it! Well, before the service was over, people had handed him nearly two hundred dollars in cash! No one in that service said anything about what he had done; he was merely seated in the congregation. The people sought him out and gave to him as God directed them. This thing really works!

The Word says God inhabits the praises of His people (see Ps. 22:3) and that He will maintain our right and our cause when we praise Him (see Ps. 9:1-4). God instructed me to use Psalm 118 when I give a praise offering. Let's examine it.

*O give thanks unto the Lord; for he is good: because his mercy endureth for ever. Let Israel now say, that his mercy endureth for ever. Let the house of Aaron now say, that his mercy endureth for ever. Let them now that fear the Lord say, that his mercy endureth for ever. I called upon the Lord in distress: the Lord answered me, and set me in a large place. The Lord is on my side.* By the time I reach this last phrase, I am about ready to shout! The Word says that if God is for you, then nobody can successfully remain your enemy (see Rom. 8:31).

*The Lord is on my side; I will not fear: what can man do unto me? The Lord taketh my part with them that help me: therefore shall I see my desire upon them that hate me. It is better to trust in the Lord than to put confidence in man. It is better to trust in the Lord than to put confidence in princes. All nations compassed me about: but in the name of the Lord will I destroy them. They compassed me about; yea, they compassed me about: but in the name of the Lord I will destroy them. They compassed me about like bees; they are quenched as the fires of thorns.* This word thorns stands for "strife."

*For in the name of the Lord I will destroy them. Thou hast thrust sore at me that I might fall: but the Lord helped me. The Lord is my strength and song, and is become my salvation. The voice of rejoicing and salvation is in the tabernacles of the righteous: the right hand of the Lord doeth valiantly. The right hand of the Lord is exalted: the right hand of the Lord doeth valiantly.* Of course, the "right hand of the Lord" is Jesus. You are praising Jesus when you do this.

*I shall not die, but live, and declare the works of the Lord. The Lord hath chastened me sore: but he hath not given me over unto death. Open to me the gates of righteousness: I will go into them, and I will praise the Lord: This gate of the Lord, into which the righteous shall enter. I will praise thee: for thou hast heard me, and art become my salvation. The stone which the builders refused is become the head stone of the corner. This is the Lord's doing; it is marvellous in our eyes. This is the day which the Lord hath made; we will rejoice and be glad in it.* You have probably heard this last verse all your life, but with the whole psalm around it and in the light of what it is for, you can see its full significance.

*Save now, I beseech thee, O Lord: O Lord, I beseech thee, send now prosperity.* Again, as in Deuteronomy 26, you are **saying** to the Lord, "Send us prosperity."

*Blessed be he that cometh in the name of the Lord: we have blessed you out of the house of the Lord. God is the Lord, which hath shewed us light: bind the sacrifice with cords, even unto the horns of the altar. Thou art my God, and I will praise thee: thou art my God, I will exalt thee. O give thanks unto the Lord; for he is good: for his mercy endureth for ever.*

When you start giving this way, just as a praise to God, things will begin to happen in your financial life. Praise is a tremendous tool in releasing the power of God. Combined with the law of giving, it is unbeatable! There is no standard return on giving as a praise to God, and it took David from sheepherder to king of Israel. Do you think God loves poverty? Read a literal Hebrew translation or the *Amplified Bible* and see the vast amount of money David put into building the Temple. It was millions of dollars! David was a prosperous man. The Bible says he was a man after God's own heart. Where do you suppose he got all his wealth? From the God of Abraham, Isaac, and Jacob who gave him the power to get wealth.

Now we have discussed these different areas of making deposits, but there are times when you can combine some of them and be even more blessed by it. I remember when I was preaching a meeting that God had said would be a turning point in my ministry. I wondered if He meant it to be a turning point the wrong way! The first evening service we had eight people. My first offering was $4.25. Naturally, I was stumped, so I went before the Lord and asked, "What in the world am I going to do?" He said, "You are going to believe **Me**! Then He showed me some things from His Word and circumstances began to pick up. The offering got all the way up to thirty-three dollars one night! I decided to send it home to my wife and the Lord said, "Thirty-three dollars won't pay your bills. If you believe My Word about tithing, if you believe that Jesus will take your money and worship Me with it, why don't you tithe now on the amount you are needing and expecting in the future offerings of this meeting? In fact, your thirty-three dollars will do just fine." That's all He said. From then on it was up to me; it involved faith on my part. You see, the money belonged to me. The Lord didn't demand that I tithe beforehand. All I actually owed in tithes was $3.30; He wanted me to give as a praise to Him for what I expected Him to do, and that is exactly what I did. I combined tithing with giving as a praise to God and the Lord blessed the meeting in every way. It started with eight people, but by Friday night people were literally sitting in the windows because there wasn't enough room to seat everyone. That meeting turned out to be the best meeting I had ever had financially up to that time. Praise the Lord! Can you see the blessings that are available in these things?

## Making Withdrawals from Your Heavenly Account

Once you realize that you have these deposits in your heavenly account, you need to learn how to make withdrawals. Colossians 1:4-6 says, *Since we heard of your faith in Christ Jesus, and of the love which ye have to all the saints, For the hope which is laid up for you in heaven, whereof ye heard before in the word of the truth of the gospel; Which is come unto you, as it is in all the world; and bringeth forth fruit.* Everything laid up for you in heaven is represented by the gospel of Jesus Christ. When you put the Word of God to work, it produces faith. *Faith cometh by hearing, and hearing by the word of God.* Faith puts spiritual law into operation, and the results are manifested here on the earth. When it is laid up in heaven, a carbon copy will take place in the earth if you will stand and act on the Word. This is how you were saved. Salvation is not waiting for you in heaven. It was provided for you and laid up in heaven; but when you believed the Word about salvation and acted on it, **it was manifested** here on earth in your life. This same principle is true in the area of finances. When a man makes deposits with God, he has a right to call upon these deposits and make withdrawals.

We have discussed God's teaching about tithing—how it is set up and how it operates. You need to learn how to receive from your tithing. When I first attended Oral Roberts University, I heard Brother Roberts speak on seed faith, and I began to realize what the Word said about giving. My wife and I decided to act on this by joining in a financial partnership with Brother Roberts, a real step of faith on our part since we had no steady income. It was during this time that we learned how to stand on the Word in the area of giving. For almost a year we gave ten dollars into this partnership each month; and every single month someone unexpectedly handed us twenty dollars. Later, we learned how to believe God more specifically, but right then we were learning the basic principles.

Let's look at Malachi 3:10 once more. There is something here I want to emphasize. *Bring ye all the tithes into the storehouse, that there may be meat in mine house, **and prove me now herewith, saith the Lord....*** God has said in many places through the Bible, "Have faith...believe Me," but here in Malachi He is saying, "Prove Me...put Me to the test!" Many Christians are looking for a sign from God as proof of His power, of His willingness to heal and do miracles in today's world. The financial realm is the only place where God gives us an opportunity to look for this sign, and it is the only place we haven't been looking! We say, "But I couldn't tell God what to do; I couldn't expect Him to bless me! It wouldn't be humble!" But what does God say? *And prove me now herewith, saith the Lord of hosts, if I will not open you the windows of heaven, and pour you out a blessing, that there shall not be room enough to receive it.*

As I was studying this one day, the phrase *windows of heaven* kept coming into my thinking, so I did some research. The phrase *windows of heaven* actually means "floodgates." It is the same word used in Genesis 7:11 where God opened the *windows of heaven* and flooded the earth. God doesn't use empty figures of speech. He means what He says! He will open the floodgates of heaven and pour out an abundant blessing on the tither. Then the next verse (Mal. 3:11) says:

*And I will rebuke the devourer for your sakes, and he shall not destroy the fruits of your ground; neither shall your vine cast her fruit before the time in the field, saith the Lord of hosts. And all nations shall call you blessed: for ye shall be a delightsome land, saith the Lord of hosts.*

Now let's discuss how to receive from your giving. Ephesians 6:8 says, *Knowing that whatsoever good thing any man doeth, the same shall he receive of the Lord, whether he be bond or free.* Whatever good thing you do to any man, you will receive the same thing from the Lord. We have just read in Malachi where God said that He would open the windows of heaven to us. Therefore, we can expect to receive from God. However, in Luke's Gospel Jesus says, *Give, and it shall be given unto you; good measure, pressed down, and shaken together, and running over, shall **men** give into your bosom. For with the same measure that ye mete withal it shall be measured to you again* (Luke 6:38). From this, we see that we also can receive from men; so the blessing is twofold. When you tithe, you receive from God above. When you give, men give into your bosom. You have it coming from all directions!

As we have already seen from Mark 10:30, Jesus promised a hundredfold return when we give for His sake and the gospel's. Using this scripture, I decided to believe for a hundredfold return when I gave my airplane as an investment in the gospel. Let me add that I didn't begin believing for a hundredfold return overnight. When I started in the ministry, a hundredfold return was more than I could fathom! I could see it in the Word of God, and I knew it was true, but it took time for my faith to develop so that these things would produce in my life. I didn't start believing for five or ten thousand dollars at a time. I began believing for the return on the first ten dollars I gave to Brother Roberts. My wife and I believed for a double return and got it every single month. But over a period of time, by meditating in the Word and **confessing** unto it, that "victory portion" of faith came alive in my heart concerning a hundredfold return.

In October 1971 I gave my airplane to the Lord. I released it, no longer claiming ownership. Then through the next few months, I continually confessed with my mouth that the withdrawal was mine, that it was on deposit in my heavenly account and would be manifested as I needed it. There were times when I would wake up in the middle of the night with fear trying to take over, trying to get me to put pressure on people, trying to get me to rent or lease or borrow. But I would fall back on the Word of God and my covenant with Him, thanking God that His Word is true and full of power. Then in January 1972 the Lord spoke and told me to whom I was to give the airplane.

At this point, I was in quite a predicament. Arrangements had been made to produce a television series, and we had no apparent capital. In addition, we had a busy schedule with no transportation. In the natural there was no way out, but by this time, we knew how deeply God was involved! Ten days later I had in my hands the exact amount I had confessed as my withdrawal. Someone I didn't even know said that God had told them to give the money. I was to put it into the ministry and not disclose from whom it came. This person wanted God to receive all the glory and He has. If you borrow from the bank, you have to answer to the banker, but when you get it from God, there are no strings attached.

Well, I had spotted another airplane and knew exactly where it was. I called the owner, and he flew it down to me. He could hardly believe it! He was a Christian too, and God had warned him three or four months earlier that he was flying around in my airplane; but he didn't think it would come to pass, so he hadn't made arrangements for one of his own. He had to do without transportation for a while! This is an exciting life! You can do what you want, but for me and my house, we will serve the Lord!

Withdrawals from the bank of heaven are accomplished through the power of agreement, the power of confession, and the power of standing expectantly on God's Word.

## The Power of Agreement

For years I knew deep down inside that there was a place in God where a man could live in victorious circumstances at all times. I knew there was total victory in Jesus, so I searched for it; but many of the people I asked about it told me that I would not be able to live this way until I got to heaven. Thank God, the Word says differently.

Matthew 18:19,20 says this: *Again I say unto you, That if two of you shall agree on earth as touching any thing that they shall ask, it shall be done for them of my Father which is in heaven. For where two or three are gathered together in my name, there am I in the midst of them.* Notice that Jesus said, *Again I say unto you.* This was important enough for Him to say more than once to these men until they realized that if they would get in agreement with one another and establish a thing, Jesus would be in the midst of them to cause it to come to pass.

You need someone to be an agreement partner with you. The most ideal situation is for a man and his wife to be in agreement. You need someone who will not relent and, once the agreement is made, will stand firm that it will come to pass. Jesus will bring even the impossible to pass if two Christians will agree **firmly** on His Word and its truth. This is the reason that in financial matters it is so important to know that you have made your heavenly deposits. It is easy to agree on the fact that something is yours when you have **already** made the deposits for it.

The prayer of agreement is a powerful prayer, and it will work when it is put to work. However, so much of the time one person will agree and another person will hope. I have prayed with people and when I finished said, "It is done and it will come to pass." Then the other person who was supposed to be agreeing with me would say, "I certainly do hope so, Brother Copeland." At that point I am forced to say, "Well, it won't. I agreed...you hoped."

When an agreement is made, both parties are firm in the fact that there is an agreed situation. When you agree with a person to pay a bill at a certain time and that person says, "I consider this bill as paid," and you say, "I certainly hope so," then that is probably as far as the situation will go until you are firm in your committal to that agreement. The other partner will not enter into it with you. It should be this firm between two Christians when they come together and believe that what they have agreed upon in the world of prosperity will come to pass. Remember, we have Jesus Christ's Word for it. It will come to pass if we refuse to relent in our agreement together.

### The Power of Confession

Jesus said in Mark 11:23, *For verily I say unto you, That whosoever shall say unto this mountain, Be thou removed, and be thou cast into the sea; and shall not doubt in his heart, but shall believe that those things which he saith shall come to pass; he shall have whatsoever he saith.* Notice the last words, *he shall have whatsoever he saith.* Faith is released with the mouth. Even our salvation is based on the confession of our mouths that Jesus Christ is our Lord (see Rom. 10:9,10). **You can have what you say!** In fact, what you are saying is exactly what you are getting now. If you are living in poverty and lack and want, change what you are saying. It will change what you have!

People continually say to me, "Brother Copeland, I cannot see what the confession of my mouth has to do with the circumstances around me." Well, I didn't understand it much when I first found out about it. Only the simple fact that Jesus said it was enough for me to begin to change my vocabulary. Since then I have learned the powerful force of the spiritual world that creates the circumstances around us is controlled by the words of the mouth. This force comes from inside us.

Jesus Himself said, *By thy words thou shalt be justified, and by thy words thou shalt be condemned* (Matt. 12:37). Words are containers. They can contain faith, love, fear, hate, or they can be totally empty. Jesus said that we would stand judgment for idle (or empty, inoperative) words (see Matt. 12:36). Remember, we said earlier that all the material substance you will ever need is already in the earth. Everything you need is already here. The confession of your mouth will cause you to possess it. God will see to that. Hebrews 3:1 says that Jesus is the Apostle and the High Priest of our confession; and Hebrews 4:14 states that we are to hold fast to our confession. We are to confess what we desire to come to pass. We don't wait until it comes to pass and then begin to confess it. In Mark 11:23, Jesus is talking about saying things that have not yet come to pass. The mountain had not yet been removed when it was spoken to. Jesus said for us to believe that those things which we say will come to pass and **then** we will have whatsoever we say. When I learned these facts, it became easy for me to confess, "I have it now.... I can see it through the eye of my faith." Once I make deposits in my heavenly account, I can say, **I have it** and then it will come to me. Sometimes it comes instantly; sometimes it comes after it is confessed several times; sometimes it comes after several days; sometimes it comes after several weeks. There have been times when it came after months of confession, but nonetheless, it came! We have God's Word for it. **It will come to pass!**

## The Power of Standing Expectantly on the Word of God

God's Word is absolutely true. There is great power in the Word. God has used the words written in the Bible to release His faith. No Word of God is void of the power it takes to cause itself to come to pass. No one has ever reached the depth of what is available in the written Word of God to the believer who will stand on God's Word as quickly and as firmly as he would the word of his lawyer or his doctor or his most trusted friend. **God's Word is God speaking to you.** God's Word is not of a private inter-pretation. It is for whosoever will! Stand on it and expect things to come to pass.

When you begin to look forward expectantly to the things God's Word promises you, you will then begin to say, "I have it." You will then begin to say, "I believe that I receive. My money is coming to me, and I will be able to be a greater blessing to the work of God's ministry, to the poor, and to the other things that I need to be involved in."

Standing on the Word of God is a spiritual activity that will bless and cause you to grow in faith and in power. James says it like this, "Faith without works is dead" (see James 2:17). He says to be a doer of the Word, an actor of the Word of God, and not a hearer only. Then he describes standing on the Word of God or looking into the Word as looking into the perfect law of liberty.

Your Heavenly Account

God's Word *always* comes to pass for the man who will stand and act on it. Your confession of God's Word will always come to pass in your life regardless of what opposition Satan puts up against it because you are confessing and expectantly standing on the Living Word of the Almighty Jehovah God. Jesus Christ is the guarantee that our covenant with God, or God's Word to us, is absolutely and eternally true. Even if heaven and earth passes away, thank God, you and I won't pass away as we stand on His Word *for His Word will not pass away!* Hebrews 1:3 states that He is upholding all things by the power of His Word. It just makes good sense then to stand on His Word if you want to be upheld financially. If you want to be upheld spiritually, get on His Word. If you want to be upheld in any area of your life, put that area on God's Word and begin to confess that you have success and victory in Jesus. It's yours!

Discipline your vocabulary. Discipline everything you do, everything you say, and everything you think to agree with what God does, what God says, and what God thinks! God will be obligated to meet your needs because of His Word—not because of your righteousness or your lack of it—but because of His Covenant that was brought into existence the day Jesus was raised from the dead. If you stand firmly on this, your needs will be met!

The Bible says that we are to owe no man anything but love (see Rom. 13:8). I will go to any lengths to love a man with the fullness of what God has given me. Suppose I had owed several thousand dollars on that airplane when God said to give it away. If that had been the case, God would not have been running my ministry; the bank would have been and I could not have given it!

How do you operate in financial situations without subordinating yourself to the world's system? What is the key that opens the channel in these things? It is available to us, but instead, all we have known is borrow, borrow, borrow! The Bible says if you will meditate in the Word of God day and night, you will have good success and deal wisely in your affairs. *The Word of God is the key.*

Begin to meditate on the Word in these areas we have discussed and give God an opportunity to tell you what to do and how to function. Remember, the rich young ruler turned and walked away. That was his biggest mistake! All he needed to do was say, "Lord, I don't understand this, but I have confidence in You. Would You please explain God's Word in this matter?" He just assumed Jesus wanted to take away everything he had, while actually Jesus was offering him the kingdom of God!

Now I want to take a moment and share something else with you. First Timothy 2:1 says that we are to pray for all men, for kings, and for all in authority. Paul wrote that we were to pray for these men *first of all*. You are to pray according to the Word of God for the men who operate around you politically. Government leaders have a great deal to do with your financial life.

The Word of God says, *[Pay] taxes to whom taxes are due* (Rom. 13:7, *Amplified*). One of the major things fouling up your life where prosperity is concerned is your bad-mouthing the government and its leaders, particularly in the area of taxation. Most people are operating in strife where their taxes are concerned, and it has a direct relationship to the government that provides our financial system. One day the Lord said, "Quit grumbling and complaining about your tax money. Pay it cheerfully the way you do your tithe and I'll bless it." From then on, my wife and I started praying over our tax money—just as we do our tithe—and we have never had a tax bill that we couldn't pay. We bless our tax money to the United States Government. That is a change, isn't it! Get strife and hard feelings toward your government out of your heart! The Word says we are to pray and give thanks for our leaders, not bad-mouth them!

Romans 13:2 says, *Whosoever therefore resisteth the power, resisteth the ordinance of God: and they that resist shall receive to themselves damnation.* After I read this in the Word, I broke my bad confession and began to pray for these men. For the first time in my life, I went to the polls and voted intelligently. No longer moved by emotions, I began to pray and seek God in voting as I did in other areas. When my attitude changed, God began to give me insight into the political affairs of this country. After approximately two weeks of praying this way, God showed me some things about the President. You see, I had opened myself to receive from God by stopping the strife in my heart. I had been very critical of the government and politicians; I griped and complained continually, but God changed my attitude. When I quit begrudging the government, God could reveal some things to me and I could receive them. This opened an area of prosperity I didn't even know existed. The Bible says these men, our civil leaders, are God's ministers for our good, that they are ordained of God. Our lack of prayer support for them has caused the problems we have seen.

As a guide for you to use in receiving from your giving in any area, let me share this little formula. It has worked consistently for us and will work for you if you commit yourself to it.

1. *Decide on the amount you need.* Be careful not to cheat yourself. God is not a skinflint. He is a giver. He is a lover. God is Love. For God so loved the world that He gave. Determine the amount you need and then be single-minded. A double-minded man can't receive anything from the Lord (see James 1:7,8).

2. *Get in agreement according to Matthew 18:19.* This is very important. The best and most powerful situation on earth is a husband and wife who can agree together in these areas. If this isn't possible in your particular case, then get together with another believer and have him join with you.

3. *Lay hold on it by faith.* Use the principles set out in Mark 11:23,24. Believe it in your heart and confess it with your mouth.

4. *Bind the devil and his forces in the name of Jesus.* You have the authority in Jesus' name to order Satan out of your financial affairs. This is *your* responsibility. Don't ask God to do it. You do it in Jesus' name. Mark 16:17, James 4:7, Ephesians 6, and the entire New Testament tells *you* to resist the devil. It is important for the husband and father to do this. It is his responsibility as spiritual head of the home.

5. *Loose the forces of heaven.* Hebrews 1:14 refers to the angels as ministering spirits "sent forth to minister for those who shall be heirs of salvation." The Bible also says that angels hearken to the Word of God (see Ps. 103:20), so when you use the Word in the name of Jesus, they are obligated to follow your command.

6. *Praise God for the answer.* Praise keeps the door of abundance wide open. The channel between you and God is clear so that you can receive from Him.

Here is an example of prayer based on these six steps:

"Father, in the name of Jesus, we ask you for $_____. We have this money in our heavenly account and we are withdrawing this amount now. We believe we receive $_____. As in Mark 11:23,24, we believe it in our hearts and confess now that it is ours in the name of Jesus. We agree that we have $_____ according to Matthew 18:19. From this day forward, we roll the care of this over on You and thank You for it. Satan, in the name of Jesus, we take authority over you; we bind your operation now and render you helpless. Ministering spirits, we charge you to go forth and cause this amount to come to us according to Hebrews 1:14. Father, we praise Your name for meeting our needs according to Your riches in glory by Christ Jesus and for multiplying our seed for sowing in the name of Jesus."

When I entered the ministry and enrolled in Oral Roberts University, my wife and I lived in an old house in Tulsa, Oklahoma, and because of business failures, we owed money in every direction. Then, as we began to grasp the principle of seed-faith giving and believing God to supply our needs, we decided to believe God to pay these debts. One night we sat down and figured what we owed. I got my checkbook and wrote out the checks that would pay these debts. We laid hands on them and prayed according to Romans 13:8, *Owe no man any thing, but to love one another.* I said, "Father, in the name of Jesus, I am putting these checks in this desk drawer and am believing You to get us out of this mess. I am looking to You for the money to pay all these debts, in the name of Jesus." I was not so *foolish* as to mail those checks before the money was in the bank. That is against the law. God will not bless fraud!

We figured to the last penny how much it would take to operate our household abundantly, even allowing for unexpected things. We wrote it down and prayed over it in the name of Jesus. I made up my mind to be single-minded from that day forward, and in less than twelve months from that night, we did not owe anything and haven't owed a penny since. God did some miraculous things during that time, and He is still doing them today! Praise God!